"The irony of laughter is it not only heals us, it's contagious, and when something is really funny, it brings tears to our eyes. I highly recommend *You're Funny* for all writers who would like to add more humor, joy, happiness, and healing energy into our world."

> – Ann Baldwin, screenwriter & author, *The Power of Dreams*; writer, *http://ahigherfrequency.blogspot.com*

"Fast. Funny. Informative. D.B. Gilles has written a delightful book about tapping into your inner funny. Read it. You'll laugh. You'll learn."

> – Matt Williams, co-creator/producer, *Roseanne*, *Home Improvement*

"Reading D.B. Gilles' *You're Funny!* is like having a friend in the business. A really good friend! He's funny, he's honest, and he speaks the truth. He tells you things you didn't even think to ask, like why writing for TV makes you fat."

> – Ellen Sandler, former co-executive producer, *Everybody Loves Raymond*; author of *The TV Writer's Workbook*

"When D.B. speaks, smart people listen. He is the Sancho Panza of writing teachers, full of worldly wisdom and common sense, and funny — you won't find a funnier book on comedy writing. Plus his advice is practical and can put money in your pocket."

> – Christopher Vogler, author of *The Writers Journey*

"Gilles' straightforward how-to teaches you all the rules you need to play this crazy comedy game. A useful and enjoyable guide for any aspiring television writer."

> – Marika Sawyer, writer, *Saturday Night Live*

"D.B. is a positive force for comedy. *You're Funny!* is a funny, entertaining, and practical guide for anyone wanting to break into the world of comedy writing."

> – Jeff Cox, writer, *Blades of Glory*

"*You're Funny!* is one of the best books available on comedy writing with a 24-carat-gold payoff – specific guidance on how to turn those skills into a profitable career."

> – Don DeMaio, American Comedy Institute

"*You're Funny!* is the first how-to handbook that ever got me laughing out loud. A longtime student of the comedy game, D.B. knows his stuff and is damned funny in passing the secrets on. A real treat."

– David McKenna, co-author of *Memo From the Story Department*

"If there ever was a book to tap in to your inner comic demon, *You're Funny* is it. Even if you don't consider yourself funny, D.B. Gilles has written a terrifically entertaining read."

– Lamar Sanders, chair, undergraduate division Kanbar Institute of Film & Television, Tisch School of the Arts, New York University

YOU'RE FUNNY!

Turn your
SENSE OF HUMOR
into a
lucrative new career

D.B. GILLES

We should consider every day lost on which we
have not danced at least once. And we should
call every truth false which was not accompanied
by at least one laugh.
– Friedrich Nietzsche

We never respect those who amuse us,
however we may smile at their comic powers.
– Marguerite Blessington

To my students, friends, and colleagues
in The Maurice Kanbar Institute of Film & Television,
Tisch School of the Arts, New York University.

And ...

To everyone who ever made me laugh.

Acknowledgments

A very special thanks to Christopher Vogler. Also to David McKenna and my agent, Michael Bourret. Major props to Denise Bongiovanni (a great stand-up) and Jack Moore (who *will* be a great stand-up) for their insights. Once again, thanks to the usual suspects, Don DeMaio and Sheldon Woodbury, for being great friends and sounding boards. I'd also like to thank the following comic minds who have given me tons of laughs over the years: George Carlin, Woody Allen, Howard Stern, Adam Carolla, David Letterman, Larry David, and Steve Allen. To my sister, Kathy, and as always, a big pug thanks to Jane Campbell, my toughest critic and best audience.

Published by Michael Wiese Productions
12400 Ventura Blvd. #1111
Studio City, CA 91604
tel. 818.379.8799 | fax 818.986.3408
mw@mwp.com | www.mwp.com

Cover Design: Johnny Ink www.johnnyink.com
Book Design: Gina Mansfield Design
Editor: Bob Somerville

Printed by McNaughton & Gunn, Inc., Saline, Michigan
Manufactured in the United States of America

Library of Congress Cataloging-in-Publication Data

Gilles, D.B.
You're funny! : turn your sense of humor into a lucrative new career / D.B. Gilles.
    p. cm.
 ISBN 978-1-932907-95-7
1. Wit and humor--Authorship. 2. Comedy--Authorship. I. Title.
 PN6149.A88G55 2011
 808.7--dc22
                                    2011002513

Mixed Sources
Product group from well-managed
forests and other controlled sources
www.fsc.org Cert no. SW-COC-002283
© 1996 Forest Stewardship Council
FSC

Table Of Contents

Foreword

You Can Say Funny Stuff, But Can You Write It?

One doesn't have a sense of humor. It has you.

— Larry Gelbart

It's a good time to be funny. And it's a *really* good time to think about trying to make a buck using your sense of humor.

Since this is a book about writing comedy, let's start with a joke:

Did you hear the one about the economic downturn and how it could affect your future as a comedy writer?

Okay. It's not a joke. I'm shooting more for paradox and irony. I mean, what better way to begin a book about comedy writing than to remind you that the economy is in a shambles. Money is tight. People are out of work. Even people *with* jobs are concerned about the future.

At the end of a frustrating day or a long week, what do most people need?

Entertainment and some laughs.

American television viewers continue to need their daily fix of comedy. After the prime time networks and cable, late night and sketch shows, audiences turn to the one channel that's all comedy.

Comedy Central continues to be an innovative force in comedy programming since its inception 20 years ago. *The Daily Show with Jon Stewart* and *The Colbert Report* are huge hits with ever-increasing ratings, audience pull, and political credibility. *South Park* is still going strong after 12 years and there are numerous comedy projects in development. Since 2006 versions of *Comedy Central* now appear in the European market including Italy, Germany, Poland, Hungary, Sweden, Italy, and the Netherlands, not to mention the United Kingdom and Ireland.

Some laugh-hungry people will go to their local Cineplex and catch a flick, especially one that'll give them some yucks.

Or, they're off to a comedy club to get a dose of live entertainment. Stand up is more popular then ever. There are over 225 comedy clubs in the United States. Some states, like Alabama, have one. Many have none. California has the most.

Los Angeles and New York continue to be the dual epicenters of stand up comedy. With both cities having more comedy venues than any other town in the world, they are the places new comedians go to cut their teeth and get their big break.

For audiences who like their stand up at home, there's *Last Comic Standing*. After taking the 2009 season off, *Last Comic Standing* returned in 2010 for its seventh season. Said an NBC network spokesman, "It has been a consistent success with both viewers and critics and we can't wait to bring it back."

It's also noteworthy that in the last several years stand up has gone global. Comics, both upcoming and established, are performing at comedy festivals throughout the world. In Scotland there's The Edinburgh Comedy Festival, which began in 2008 as an offshoot of the renowned Edinburgh Festival Fringe, and The Glascow Comedy Festival.

In Spain: The Barcelona International Comedy Festival. South Africa offers The Cape Town Comedy Festival.

There's The Melbourne International Comedy Festival in Australia, and in that same corner of the planet, The New Zealand International Comedy Festival.

In Dublin, The Bulmers International Comedy Festival reigns supreme. Hong Kong and Singapore both have International Comedy Festivals. Canada has The Global Comedy Fest in Vancouver and in Montreal, The Just For Laughs Comedy Festival, as well as The Montreal International Comedy Festival. Plus The Halifax Comedy Festival in Nova Scotia.

Upper echelon comedians are selling out huge venues and earning multi-millions. Last year the following comics were the Top 10 earning comedians: Jerry Seinfeld, Chris Rock, Jeff Dunham, Dane Cook, George Lopez, Howie Mandel, Larry The Cable Guy, Jeff Foxworthy, Terry Fator, and Russell Peters.

In the quest for laughs, people also have the choice of going to their computers to find entertainment and chuckles on innumerable websites ranging from short films on *Funny Or Die*, parody at *The Onion*, amazing wit at *drmardy.com* and funny news (and not news) from *Fark.com*.

History tells us that when times are tough, people want to laugh. They *need* to laugh.

That's where you come in.

You have the ability to amuse people in your personal life. Now you're ready to see if you can get *more* from your sense of humor than laughs.

Let's talk about you for a moment. Maybe you're not all that "happy" yourself. You don't like your job anymore (or maybe you never did). Despite college and a degree (or two) you now realize you went into the wrong profession. Or maybe it was right for you at one time, but not anymore.

Even if you've made good money, you're, well, miserable. Too extreme a word? Okay. Unhappy. Dissatisfied. Bored. Frustrated. All of the above?

Whatever your state of mind, and whatever your reason for taking the leap from funny person with friends, family and co-workers, to someone who earns money from your talent, you're starting the journey at an opportune time.

A whole new, expansive audience is waiting for you to make them laugh.

Let's find out the best way for you to do this.

How to Know for Sure You Should be Writing Comedy

You know you're a comedy writer if you would much rather be playing "Grand Theft Auto" than be in a book club discussing the works of Teilhard de Chardin. Instead of *going* to therapy, you ridicule people who do. You can't get through a day without trying to make every person you know laugh. You believe that your sense of humor can get you out of any awkward situation. You joined "Second Life," where you created not only a Second Life, but a *Second* Second Life and have contemplated starting a *Third* Second Life.

If you're a guy, you get little if any exercise and spend too much time indoors — usually online — and you've visited way too many porn sites. You've subscribed to *Fangoria* since you were a kid, still have every issue, and look forward to passing your collection on to your son and watching your favorite splatter films with him. You have to think twice about whether you would rather make a woman laugh or have sex with her.

If you're a woman, you worry that you'll never find Mr. Right because none of the dullards you meet get your sense of humor. On a date, you have to restrain yourself from making wisecracks and clever observations for fear that the guy will resent that you're funnier than he is. You reject the historically accepted female virtues of modesty and submission in favor of telling a good dick joke. You have to hide the fact that you love gross-out humor, especially fart and bodily function jokes. You have to think twice about whether you would rather make a guy laugh or have sex with him.

Only kidding!

Well, not really. Comedy writers do tend to be a little strange, weird, and off-the-wall. I should know. I'm one of them. Therapy helps. A little.

PART 1

Two Jews Walk Into a Bar: Comedy Writing Basics

I regard the writing of humor as a supreme artistic challenge.

— Herman Wouk

Introduction

Somebody Laughed

*Humor is an affirmation of dignity, a declaration
of man's superiority to all that befalls him.*

— Romain Gary

There was a moment in your life when you acknowledged to yourself that you were funny. Maybe you were trying to be funny. Maybe
you weren't. Maybe it just slipped out.

But somebody laughed.

Or giggled.

Perhaps someone just smiled.

It might have happened when you were in second grade or fresh-
man year in high school, or when you were a senior in college.
You did or said something that got a rise out of your teacher and
snickers from your classmates.

Or it could have happened when you were out of school and into
a career when you got that first reaction from a coworker at the
photocopy machine.

Maybe your boss laughed at something you blurted out at a meeting. Maybe a group of people laughed at what you said while you
were in an elevator. Or you realized that a thought you had or a remark that slipped out was incredibly witty or clever or, well, funny.

Perhaps you had a knack for making cute, endearing remarks that
made your relatives laugh at family gatherings.

You liked the feeling. Maybe you even loved it. But one thing for
sure: You knew deep down that you needed to hear that laughter.
So you tried to get your laughs wherever you could. Depending
upon how shy you were, maybe you limited it to your siblings or

3

parents. You'd do goofy stuff or say nutty things and get your laugh fix from your family.

Once you had them in the palm of your hand, you may have decided to test the waters outside the safety of your home. So there was school or the sports teams you played on or the clubs you joined. The people here were a tougher audience. Maybe the silly things you did at home were too easy. You had to be more creative. So you'd take a shot. Sometimes you'd get the laugh. Other times you'd crash and burn.

Crashing and burning was probably more the norm. But on the days when you got the laugh, it made the failures worthwhile. Getting the laughs did something to you. Maybe it built up your confidence. Made you feel cool. Hip.

Perhaps your sense of humor got you into a more high-profile crowd. If you're a guy, maybe it got you a cuter girl. If you're a girl, maybe it got you a better-looking guy. But you were too young to be thinking about what to do with this talent you had to make people laugh. Maybe you were too young to even realize it was a talent.

All you knew was that you liked making people laugh and you got a lot of satisfaction from doing it.

4

Maybe it was enough just to make your friends and family laugh. Maybe people liked being around you because they knew you were the funny guy or the funny girl.

Or maybe you didn't do anything. You just kept saying funny things and getting laughs. You'd reached the point where you *knew* you were funny. It was expected of you and you embraced that feeling, whether at work, school or, for that matter, anywhere.

Then one day it hit you. You were watching a lousy sitcom or a mediocre sketch on *Saturday Night Live* or you had just laid out twenty bucks at your local cineplex for a comedy with hardly any laughs. Then, as if possessed by the ghost of Groucho Marx, you thought or uttered seven words that would change your life:

"I could write funnier stuff than that."

That's when you hit your first brick wall. Could you *really write* funnier stuff than that? You'd never tried to write anything funny before. Not for real. Maybe in high school or college you channeled your comedic ability into a satirical essay for an English class or you dashed out a humor column in the school paper. You might've written a couple of skits for a school talent show.

But you never, *not ever*, tried to write a sketch or an episode for your favorite sit-com or a Top 10 list a la David Letterman.

And you definitely never wrote a joke. The only jokes you told were the ones you heard from other people, just like everyone else. But to actually *write* an original joke? No way had you tried that. And to actually create a funny sketch that would be on a par with the best of *SCTV*, *Mr.Show*, or *Kids in the Hall*?

No way had you tried that.

And to write an episode of your favorite sitcom? You definitely never tried that.

And if you had the idea of being a stand-up comic, of creating a persona and of writing an "act" — No way in hell did you ever try that. (You weren't even sure what an "act" meant.)

Once you accepted the fact that you were going from being the funniest person in your crowd to being a comedy writer, you had one really large question: *How do I go about doing it?*

That's where I can help.

If you're interested in breaking into the world of sitcom writing, I'll take you step-by-step through the process of selecting the right show to write a script for, from vague idea to outline to first draft to second draft to polish. If sketch writing is your thing, I'll give you suggestions and tips on avoiding the pitfalls that even the best-written sketches fall victim to. If it's writing for late night television, writing screenplays, parody, short humor for magazines, or humorous fiction, I'll walk you through the steps.

Maybe you're not sure what you want to do, or perhaps you want to do everything. I'll help you learn how to think like a professional comedy writer.

First you'll have to decide what kind of comedy writer you are.

a quick lesson

There are three types of humor: verbal, visual, and physical.

Most visual and physical humor fits into the following categories: An object or person can become funny by being in an unusual place, behaving in an unusual way, or being the wrong size (*Ratatouille*; *Shallow Hal*; *The Three Stooges*, *Shrek*; *Me, Myself and Irene*; *Harvey*).

Verbal humor relies strictly on a person's wit (Bill Maher, Adam Carolla, Dennis Miller, and brilliantly written sitcoms like *Seinfeld, Cheers, Arrested Development, The Office, Taxi, Frasier*).

Television shows like *The Simpsons* and *Family Guy* rely on all three.

a quick exercise

Make a list of your favorite sitcoms and film comedies, and define their humor.

chapter 1

Laughs, Giggles, Yucks, and Appreciative Nods

A joke is a very serious thing.

— Winston Churchill

Before you can write funny stuff, you need to have an understanding of the variations of humor.

To wit:

It was one of the first comedy-writing classes I'd ever taught, but nobody was laughing.

As I often do to make a point, I cracked a joke. Not a conventional joke that gets told over and over again as it's passed from one person to another, but something original. It was an off-the-cuff one-liner about a current political event.

The problem was that not one of the 17 people in the class was laughing.

There were none of the usual giggles, yucks, smirks, chuckles, or even half-smiles. Their faces stared back at me in silence. It was awkward. I couldn't tell if they weren't getting the joke because it was topical or if it just wasn't funny.

One of the things I emphasize in my classes is the value of keeping current. I point out that smart, informed people tend to be funnier than those who aren't. Had they read a newspaper, gone online to catch some news, or watched *The Daily Show* the night before, they might have gotten my joke.

On the other hand, I've also encountered plenty of extremely funny individuals — like my cousin Randy — who couldn't pass a current events test if their lives depended on it. But Randy's been cracking people up with his quick wit since middle school.

red back at them, disappointed that my line had gone over their heads. I was sure what I'd said was funny and very worthy of a reaction. I've done this long enough to realize when something I say misses the mark.

Then I saw one girl in the back of the classroom nodding her head, and I felt vindicated. I had *reached* her. She *got* the joke. Her face was expressionless. She wasn't even close to a smile. But she had given me the lowest form of approval on the food chain of funny for a clever remark: The Appreciative Nod.

It's nowhere near as satisfying as having people laugh so hard that they start to cry or can barely catch their breath. But it's enough to give you your laugh fix for the moment.

The Appreciative Nod is where it starts for those of us who like (or need) to make people laugh. Following close behind is The Approving Smile, which is actually better than an appreciative nod because there's great comfort in seeing someone smile. Go back to your childhood when Mom or Dad smiled at some cute, comical thing you did. You saw that smile of approbation and you felt all warm and fuzzy.

Ask most women and they'll tell you that they prefer a guy who makes them laugh. And most men will say they prefer a woman with a good sense of humor. If you're a man, ask the women you know how many great-looking, studly, or rich guys they dumped because they were boring, i.e., not especially funny.

In a scientific study concentrating on finding out what people laugh at, using a 1,200-person focus group, Robert R. Provine, professor of psychology at the University of Maryland, came to several conclusions:

- While both sexes laugh a lot, females laugh more.

- In cross-gender conversations, females laughed 126% more than their male counterparts.

- Women tend to do the most laughing, while males tend to do the most laugh-getting.

- Across cultures, men seem to be the main instigators of humor, a tendency that begins in early childhood.

- The laughter of the female is the critical index of the health of a relationship.

What does this mean? In lay terms, a guy who can say funny things will do better with most women — provided, of course, that he doesn't meet a woman who requires a higher consciousness of humor. Being witty and strikingly original enters the picture now. Humorwise, it's what separates the men from the boys. Women with a good sense of humor expect smart, imaginative men.

There's a famous story about the playwright Charles MacArthur and his wife, legendary actress Helen Hayes. On the night they met at a party, he gave her a handful of peanuts and said, "I wish they were emeralds." Years later, after they'd been married for decades and he had enjoyed great success, he handed her a handful of emeralds and said, "I wish they were peanuts."

Romantic? Yes. Sentimental? Yes. Clever? Big yes. But if you're someone who appreciates humor, it's an incredibly witty way for a man to tell and show a woman he loves her.

In the food chain of funny, getting beyond appreciative nods and approving smiles is the next challenge.

Welcome to The Shake-Your-Head Giggle. This is when you say something off-the-wall, but not too crazy — just enough to get a positive reaction from your prudish sister or archconservative religious uncle. The Shake-Your-Head Giggle might also be followed by a comment such as, "You're terrible" or "I can't believe you said that."

Next is The Sustained Laugh. Not quite an enthusiastic outburst, but a genuine reaction from the heart usually accompanied with a big smile and the nodding (or shaking back and forth) of the head.

Then comes the big one!

The Killer Laugh. The one where people laugh uncontrollably to the point of tears and physical pain, i.e., laughing till it hurts. Whether you're a stand-up comic or Greg the wacky accountant in payroll, The Killer Laugh is what you live for.

As I said earlier, everyone can't tell a joke. But it's fair to assume that even the dullest, most humorless people have tried to tell a joke and gotten a blank stare or an awkward "I don't get it." If this happened every time they told a joke, those with self-awareness most likely concluded that joke-telling wasn't their forte. And unless they were masochists, they resolved never to do it again.

You Learn Fast If You're Not Good at Telling Jokes

And you learn equally fast if you're not good at writing funny lines, dialogue, and situations. Someone reading your lines either laughs or not.

The toughest decision you have to make if you want to write comedy is if you have the comic chops to do it.

Steve Allen, humorist and pioneer talk show host, was asked why he was able to say something instantly funny time and time again. His response was, "It might take the average person 37 seconds to think of something funny to say, but that's too long. Humor has to be immediate."

The French have an expression, *l'esprit de l'escalier*, or "the wit of the staircase," which is the tendency to think of a quick comeback only after it's too late to say it. There are only so many stony silences you can take before deciding to keep your mouth shut.

The funniest people I know are all quick. Within one second they're able to say something funny. And they do it over and over again. Ironically, most of them aren't comedy writers. They're regular people. And many of the comedy writers I know are hilarious on the page, but in real life are kind of, well, boring and anything but quick.

The most important thing to understand is to be original. Don't make the same joke or say the same line that everyone else is saying.

Four hundred years ago, satirist Jonathan Swift said this more succinctly: "What some people invent the rest enlarge."

Periodically, catchphrases and expressions trickle down into the pop culture vernacular, usually from the street, television, movies, or commercials.

Here are a few that had their time in the sun:

- "Not that there's anything wrong with being gay."
- "Denial is a river in Egypt."
- "Thank you for sharing."
- "Oh my God."
- "Make my day."
- "Too much information."
- "Don't go there."
- "Whazzzzuupppp?"
- "Get a life."

- "Hated it!"

- "Excuuuussse me."

- "That doesn't make me a bad person."

- "Yada yada yada!" (which, believe it or not, is in the dictionary!)

- "Duh!"

- "No you di'nt!"

How many times have you heard the following lines in a screenplay? "She's no rocket scientist," or "It's not rocket science." I've heard those lines or variations on those lines so many times it makes me cringe. They represent bad writing and lack of imagination. The only time the line ever truly worked, after the first time, was in a nifty little comedy from 1985 called *Moving Violations*, starring John Murray (Bill's brother) and Jennifer Tilly (Meg's sister).

It went something like this:

John Murray's character: "You're not a rocket scientist."

Jennifer Tilly's character: "Actually, I am."

Again, fill whatever you're writing with original humor and steer clear of the obvious, clichéd, and trite.

Why are some people funnier than others? Why are some screenplays funnier than others? Why do some jokes work and others don't?

E. B. White said it best: "Analyzing humor is like dissecting a frog. Few people are interested and the frog dies."

I mean, it's not rocket science, right?

Freud on Funny

I Don't Get It

In Sigmund Freud's *Jokes and Their Relation to the Unconscious,* he writes, "... our brain has certain specifications upon which laughter can be incited; however, similar to our distinct personalities, one's sense of humor is entirely dependent on their individual being and the tendencies specific to their varied states of consciousness."

Practically speaking, this is why some people get a joke and others don't. Why you laughed throughout *Hot Tub Time Machine* and your significant other sat there stone-faced. Why some people think Carrot Top or Dane Cook is amazing and others wonder why they have successful careers. Think of all the sitcoms, film comedies, and comedians you like and your friends don't, and remember what Freud says.

To each, his own. Not my cup of tea. I don't get it.

It will be the same way with whatever form of comedy you write. Some people will get it and others won't. The only difference is that as you pursue a writing career, it's crucial that the *right* people get it.

chapter 2

If You're *out* of Touch, You Won't Get *in* the Door

*Life literally abounds in comedy if you
just look around you.*

— Mel Brooks

Smart, informed writers write funnier stuff than people who don't know what's going on in the world. If you're not a news junkie, you'd better become one.

Keep current with what's happening in our country and around our planet. Read newspapers for national and international news; watch your local TV news, too. You never know where you're going to find material. If you're too cheap to buy newspapers, go online; almost every newspaper is free for the viewing. I suggest concentrating on papers in New York, Los Angeles, and Washington.

Because I live in New York I read *The New York Times* for serious news and *The New York Post* for pop culture and oddball human-interest stories.

Pay even closer attention to pop culture news. Think of all the jokes that have been written about Paris Hilton, Lindsay Lohan, Britney Spears, and Sarah Palin, as well as their dysfunctional families. If you look at *People* magazine or *Us* and you've never heard of most of the actors, singers, or entertainers on the cover, you're out of touch.

There's always someone new on the horizon to make fun of.

Read as many online sites about Hollywood personalities as you can, because these are the people you'll be drawing humor from.

Here are some you should bookmark:

- *Perez Hilton*
- Nikki Fincke's *Deadline Hollywood*
- *Popculturemadness*
- *TMZ*
- *The Hollywood Gossip*
- *The Superficial*
- *Gawker*
- *E! Online*
- *TV Squad*
- *PopSugar*
- *Laineygossip*
- *I'm Bringing Blogging Back*
- *The Hollywood Grind*
- *Dlisted*
- *Bricksandstonesgossip*
- *Hilaryshepard*
- *National Enquirer*

You should also watch every pop culture TV news show. DVR them. Fastforward through stuff that's remote, but take in the material that's ripe for ridicule.

- *The Soup*
- *E!Online*
- *TMZ*
- *E! Entertainment*
- *Access Hollywood*
- *The Insider*
- *Entertainment Tonight*

And definitely check out the following political websites and blogs even if they're not on your side.

- *The Huffington Post*
- *The Daily Kos*
- *The Drudge Report* (which connects you to many other news links and columns)
- *Wonkette*
- *Politico*
- *Indecisionforever.com*
- *Salon*

- *The Hill*
- *RealClearPolitics*
- *TalkingPointsMemo*
- *HotAir*
- *Crooks and Liars*

And of course *The Daily Show with Jon Stewart* and *The Colbert Report*.

Whatever your politics, by exposing yourself to what left- and right-wing columnists are writing about, you'll be more connected to what's going on in the world. But unlike the average person who reads the news for information, you will be looking for material. The more you learn every day, the more you'll have to draw on for material.

You also need to ask yourself how much you really know about comedy. Are you funny by instinct or are you well-schooled in the underlying nature of comedy?

It's a big plus to be funny by instinct, but that can only get you so far. It's like being a natural athlete. Somebody lucks out in the genetic lottery, but without the proper coaching and training, he won't learn how to refine his natural God-given abilities.

Adolescent boys who can't get attention from girls with their looks or intelligence or by excelling at sports resort to goofball antics either physical or verbal. But that only goes so far and lasts so long. The kid whose talent is shoving a slice of pizza up his nose will be trumped by the boy who has figured out that girls get bored quickly with silliness and prefer someone who can amuse them with wit.

15

If you're going to take the plunge and compete in the world of comedy writing, it's essential that you do as my father liked to say: "Smarten up."

One way to do this is to get a handle on what laughter is all about.

People laugh for many reasons: when they're nervous, excited, tense, happy, tricked by someone, or simply because someone else is laughing or crying. In the past, laughter was considered an unsocial, sinister behavior. In the 18th century, Lord Chesterfield, writing to his son, said, "...there is nothing so illiberal, and so ill-bred, as audible laughter."

According to Oliver Goldsmith, laughter was the expression of "the vacant mind" and John Ray likened it to "the hiccup of a fool."

Fortunately, laughter is way more cool these days. There will always be an audience for laughter. People will pay to bring laughter into their lives.

If you want to be the recipient of their money, you have to educate yourself so you can discover the road that's right for you.

The R Word

New writers of any genre hate to rewrite. They don't understand its value. The tendency of most people taking their baby steps as writers is to get it out and assume that it's good.

It usually isn't. And when it comes to comedy, not being good means that it's not funny enough.

It might have a few laughs, but not enough. It might have more than a few laughs, but the story or situation is weak and the jokes don't make sense. It might have lots of laughs and the story is strong, but it can still be better, i.e., funnier.

If you have one laugh on a page, try to get two or three. If you have two laughs on a page, aim for four or five.

If you're satisfied that you have enough laughs, check the structure. Does the story get started too late? Do you go off on an unnecessary tangent midway? Can the ending be better? Funnier?

Once you understand that rewriting is second nature, you've crossed a major threshold.

a quick lesson

Before You Break the Rules, Learn the Rules

Ultimately, all forms of comedy writing are about learning the form and formula.

There is a right way to structure a joke, monologue, scene, TV script, and screenplay. Once you've decided the kind of comedy writing you're going to pursue, then it's a matter of learning the rules and necessary craft required. If you want to go "out of the box," do it once you've mastered the rules.

Musicians who wind up playing jazz had to learn the musical scales first before they played their first riff.

.

chapter 3

WWLD
The Genius of Larry David

Humor is a social lubricant that helps us
get over some of the bad spots.

— Steve Allen

A guy who smells really awful lives in my apartment building. He's pleasant enough and I found out he's a lawyer for the City of New York. Problem is that he smells so bad he stinks up the elevator. This guy is ripe.

He lives five floors below me.

What has happened on a number of occasions is that we've ridden up together in the elevator from the lobby and he gets off on his floor; then someone gets in the elevator on a floor between mine and his, and the person walks into an invisible stench of bubonic plague proportion and naturally assumes that I'm the one who stinks.

This is a Larry David moment. What I call "assumed guilt" or "presumed culpability."

Larry David struck comedy gold when he and Jerry Seinfeld created *Seinfeld*. His gift for finding humor in the minutiae of life struck a chord with audiences. He mined this to even greater success in his HBO series *Curb Your Enthusiasm*.

Another thing Larry's character on *Curb* experiences is the innocent or casual action that causes a problem (or a chain of problems) for him or someone else. There's also the self-serving behavior that becomes the catalyst for a crisis that shouldn't have happened but spirals out of control.

These situations don't just happen to Larry's character in *Curb*. They happen to us all. Not every day or every week or every month. Most people don't give these experiences much thought beyond the moment they happen, but as a comedy writer, you should.

Once I was buying a couple of things in a drugstore. There were two people ahead of me. The cashier sneezed and a gigantic wad of greenish snot appeared in her left nostril. It was gross. She wasn't aware of it. As she waited on the two people ahead of me, I wondered if she would realize the snot was there and wipe it off. She didn't. She just didn't know it was there.

It's now my turn. Ironically, I was buying a box of Kleenex. She rings it up and sets the box down, and then the cashier next to her subtly points at her nose and my cashier takes her right hand and proceeds to remove the snot from her nose. Unfortunately, it's now on her right finger. She picks up my pristine box of Kleenex with the hand *with the snot finger* and puts it in a bag. The snot was now transferred to my Kleenex box. I didn't want to take that box. It felt tainted, but I didn't have the heart to ask her for another one. So I took it, covered with snot. When I got home I took a Kleenex from the box and wiped it off. Dramatic irony.

Is that a scene from *Curb Your Enthusiasm* or what?

What would Larry David have done with that incident?

Try to remember experiences like this and start being aware of those that crop up.

Larry David has had an illustrious career by taking situations and putting his particular spin on them. Long before I started watching either show, I was experiencing these oddball situations (as I imagine you and everyone else have). But I never did anything with them, other than tell an amusing story or anecdote.

Larry David made me realize the importance of looking for the things in our lives that embarrass us and the things that we do that put us in awkward or cringe-worthy situations.

I am constantly on the lookout for things that I can use in my own writing. And as a teacher I'm always looking for examples to share with my students.

Recently, I was in a restaurant having drinks and appetizers with a friend. Our waitress was efficient but unfriendly. Not rude, but totally charmless. She looked at me as if I had killed her cat and eaten it. But as I said, she was efficient. I left her a decent tip, but I was angry that she hadn't been friendlier. I like a friendly waiter or waitress. Even if the smile and attitude is bullshit, in the handful of seconds she spends with a customer she should be pleasant and charming. I should point out that this was in a very nice restaurant.

Two days later I was in a Starbucks. The same waitress sat as a customer at the next table with two friends. I'm sure she wouldn't have remembered me. In the 20 minutes or so she was there, she was as smiling and friendly as can be with her friends. The more she smiled and laughed and behaved nicely, the more I wanted to go over to her and tell her that she should behave that way when she's waiting tables.

I asked myself: What would Larry David do with this?

Another question arises: When did Larry David discover this voice?

Seinfeld aired in 1989. Larry David was 42. Did he have the point of view that made him famous at 20 or 30 or 35? Or was it something that developed gradually throughout his career as a stand-up comic, writer, and performer, something that was born when he and Jerry Seinfeld got their TV deal?

This is not to say that if you don't find the right course of action for yourself, you'll be a failure. There have been thousands of comedy writers who have made wonderful livings and led creative, imaginative lives, and you may be one of them.

But that doesn't mean that your long-term goal shouldn't be to find and nurture your special niche.

a viewing exercise

Examine the work of the following unique writers (and performers) of past and present generations: Charlie Chaplin, Howard Stern, Judd Apatow, Buster Keaton, Adam Carolla, Woody Allen, W. C. Fields, Laurel and Hardy (Stan Laurel was the creative force behind their act), Mel Brooks, and Jonathan Winters. Pinpoint what made them unique, then look into yourself and make a list of five things that make you unique and that can serve as the basis of something funny to write.

Something You Should Know That's Not Big Enough to Deserve Its Own Chapter

From One Laugh Whore to Another

By definition, a laugh whore is someone with an overwhelming desire to be funny. If you're reading this now, you probably are one. It's cool. I am too.

From the moment you decide to try to write comedy for a living, your life as the funny guy or girl with your friends, family, and coworkers will be different.

You will be competing with other funny men and women who've taken the leap into the real world. You will discover that you are funnier than some and that others are funnier than you. Obviously, it's the people who are funnier than you that you have to worry about.

No matter what niche you decide to pursue, besides encountering people who are funnier than you, you'll also run into people who work harder at their craft than you. These people will be your nemesis. They can and will get into your head. If you're working two hours a day, they're working six. You're going out on weekends and having fun; they're at home writing, or if they're stand-up comics, they're out at comedy clubs trying to get stage time every night and at more than one club per night. Somebody's taking classes and you're playing video games.

Your inherent nature will cause you to continue to try to make the people in your life laugh. But don't go overboard. Getting your laugh whore needs met can no longer be a priority. You will need to put your creative energy into your work.

You're done putting on a puppet show. As the old showbiz saying goes ...

Save it for the performance!

THE MASTERS SPEAK

The only honest art form is laughter, comedy. You can't fake it.... Try to fake three laughs in an hour — ha ha ha ha ha — they'll take you away, man. You can't.

— Lenny Bruce

Comedy has to be done en clair. You can't blunt the edge of wit or the point of satire with obscurity. Try to imagine a famous witty saying that is not immediately clear.

— James Thurber

Perhaps I know best why it is man alone who laughs; he alone suffers so deeply that he had to invent laughter.

— Friedrich Nietzsche

PART 2

Short Humor, Parody, and Satire

Satire is a lesson, parody is a game.

— Vladimir Nabokov

23

chapter 4

Start Small With Short Humor and Blogs

Humor is reason gone mad.

— Groucho Marx

Before you run in a marathon, take a brisk walk around the block. Short humor won't make you rich, but it can be a way of testing the water in your new comedy-writing career.

I tell people who want to be playwrights to start by writing a five-page scene, then move up to a 10-minute play (which means no more than 10 pages). From there they tackle a few variations of a one-act play: first 15-20 pages, then 30 pages, then a long one-act play of 60 pages. Then it's time to write the full-length play (80 pages and up).

It stands to reason that before taking on a sketch (3-5 pages), TV spec script (35 pages) or a full-length screenplay (110 pages), it might be smart to write something less than one page.

What is a short humor piece?

Think of it as something between 500 and 1,000 words that would appear in *The Onion*, *The New Yorker*, *The New York Times* op-ed page, *The Huffington Post*, and numerous periodicals of all tastes and subjects. And of course there's *Mad Magazine* and *National Lampoon*.

New York Times columnist Maureen Dowd has a unique comedic voice. She wrote a piece relating tensions in North Korea to the characters in *Mean Girls*.

Woody Allen has been publishing short pieces in *The New Yorker* since the 1960s. Think of the work of David Sedaris. Steve Martin also has a side career of writing short humor pieces (not to mention plays and novels). To get a sampling of their work, Google *The New Yorker* and go to their archives.

Short humor could also be a comical essay for *Esquire*, *Cosmopolitan*, *Playboy*, or any number of men's and women's magazines, not necessarily only humor magazines. The Internet is filled with e-zines and websites that are looking for material. They may not pay anything, but you're getting a credit and exposure.

The key to short humor is, well, to keep it short.

If you write something that will fill one page in a mainstream magazine, you have a better chance of selling it. Same with an op-ed piece for *The New York Times*. Perhaps two or three times a month you'll see something amusing there and they're typically less than 500 words.

Less is more is the case with virtually all writing, but even more so with the short stuff.

I'm not talking about short stories. They are an entirely different thing. Other than in oddball contests where people are asked to write a short-short story, most short stories go over that 1,000 limit I mentioned.

Below is a short humor piece that I wrote for *The New York Times*.

How to Run a Network in 12 Easy Steps

At a secret location high in the Hollywood Hills, a unique support group meets once a week to share the pain of a specialized dysfunction that began during the latter half of the 20th century.

Its abbreviation is OCPD, otherwise known as Obsessive Compulsive Programming Disorder. Its victims are past and present individuals who have run a network and found themselves in the position of deciding what gets on and what doesn't.

Here, smuggled out of the meeting place, is the official 12-Step Program agenda for OCPD victims:

(1). Have the conviction to cancel sitcoms that aren't funny, to renew what *is* funny, and to know the difference.

(2). Have the strength not to give Kelsey Grammar another sitcom. He was unforgettable as Frasier and will always be associated with the character no matter how hard he tries not to be.

(3). Have the faith to resist all inclinations to take genuinely fresh and original concepts and develop them into finished products that only a business major could love.

(4). Have the self-confidence to not even think about ripping off *Keeping Up With the Kardashians*.

(5). Have the courage to use your political contacts to pass federal legislation that would bar any further sitcoms dealing with mismatched roommates, single moms, divorced dads, or oddly blended families.

(6). Have the nerve to develop programs about flesh-and-blood, recognizable human beings (even if they are animated or aliens).

(7). Have the self-assurance to eliminate from your vocabulary the words "tried" and "true" (except when used in the following context: "I tried to watch *Hank* and it's *true* — it sucked").

(8). Have the boldness to say yes to intelligent, witty, cerebral comedies that won't ever be in the Top 10 or Top 20 or even the Top 30 and probably won't generate big advertising bucks and may barely break even, but just might draw in an audience so turned off to most of what's on that it could start a trend and help you take pride in bringing wit back to the boob tube.

27

(9). Have the assertiveness to greenlight programs for audiences over 50. Millions of high-end baby boomers who were couch potatoes before the term was even invented are channel-surfing every night. They're tired of watching the icons of their youth trashed on *E!'s True Hollywood Story*, crop circle theories on the Discovery Channel, and Bill O'Reilly's nightly attempt to be tougher than Mike Wallace.

(10). Have the integrity to undo the damage your predecessors have done to children by eliminating violence and blatant sexual innuendo that has certainly gotten some of these people really nasty spots in Hell. Always remember: Satan is waiting.

(11). Have the fortitude to ignore focus groups, demographics, and overeducated, over-opinionated experts and instead ask the person who cleans your office, or delivers your wine, or drops off your FedEx packages what they think. And never, *ever* forget that these are called "regular" people, who watch TV to relax at the end of a hard day.

(12). Have the wisdom, should you find a "regular" person whose insights are right on the money, to resist all urges to hire him or her as a vice president.

Just under 550 words. It has some amusing points. I was poking fun (or taking aim) at network programmers. I made my point and did so with humor.

Now you try it.

reading assignment

Google the following. Look at the construction and pacing of the various essays. What are the authors' points of view? Are they clear? Are they clever? Are they amusing?

- Larry David's *New York Times* op-ed piece: "My War"
- *The Borowitz Report* by Andy Borowitz
- Maureen Dowd's *New York Times* op-ed piece: "To Tweet or Not to Tweet"
- Will Durst (*willdurst.com*)
- Carl Hiaasen's columns in *The Miami Herald*
- Dave Barry (*davebarry.com*)
- Woody Allen's *New Yorker* pieces: "Tails of Manhattan," "Think Hard, It'll Come to You," and "Udder Madness"
- Madeleine Begun Kane (*madekane.com*)
- Bill Shein (*reasongonemad.com*)
- Tom Purcell (*tompurcell.com*)

writing assignment no. 1

Come up with 10 ideas for a short humor piece. Choose the one you like best and write an essay of 500-750 words. 12 pt. Courier. Double-spaced, which equals three pages.

writing assignment no. 2

Write a satiric opinion piece on something that irritates you. 500-750 words.

writing assignment no. 3

Write a satirical essay for *The Onion*. Either go online and check out their website or if you have access to the paper, study it cover to cover. Look at the length of the pieces. Most are short. Some are longer. Some work very well; some don't. Ask yourself why you laughed at some and didn't at others. Then write one.

Something You Should Know That's Not Big Enough to Deserve Its Own Chapter

Why Blogs Were Meant for Fledgling Comedy Writers

As far as I'm concerned there are two kinds of blogs: those that offer information on learning or improving on a skill, and those that are chronicles of a person's life.

Some of the latter are entertaining as hell and are fun to read. Many of these are directed at a niche audience. New moms, new dads, retirees, cooks, tell-alls about different professions. However, most of these kinds of blogs are about the minutiae of someone's life, i.e., "I found a bug in my hamburger today," or "Checked out the campus of Penn State today," or "Last night's episode of *Big Bang Theory* was awesome."

29

Who reads these things I don't know, but I do know that the blogs I read are for entertainment and education in areas I'm interested in: movies, television, and cooking.

People who want to begin their comedy-writing career with short humor should start a blog. They're easy to construct and free. Find your niche and start posting short pieces. Give yourself the goal of writing at least two posts a week, maybe three. Unless you're having an incredibly busy week, don't back away from this schedule.

It's all about the discipline. You're learning to write short humor. The best way to learn is to do it. The more of them you write, the better you'll get. Some will be superb, some will suck, and the rest will be somewhere in between.

With each blog post you write, you'll get better and more comfortable putting your thoughts and ideas on paper.

If your blog topic is interesting, colorful, entertaining, and provides information to help readers develop or improve a skill, it'll catch on.

The ultimate goal of a blog for anyone seriously trying to be a comedy writer should be to create a solid Internet platform of readership in order to turn your blog into a book.

In the case of Julie Powell, her blog *The Julie/Julia Project* became not only a book, but also a movie: *Julie & Julia*.

Steve Dublanica, a waiter, started a blog called *Waiter Rant*, which described the ups and downs of being a waiter. It resulted in a best-seller of the same name.

Even if you don't achieve results like them, what you will gain is experience in writing and it will prepare you to move on to longer projects.

Save it for the performance!

chapter 5

Getting in Touch With Your Inner Oscar Wilde

Consistency is the last refuge of the unimaginative.

— Oscar Wilde

Do you know what satire is? Parody? Are they the same, fairly close in meaning, or totally different? What's a lampoon? A spoof? What is farce?

I'll pretend you don't know. Don't bother doing a quick Google search. I'll tell you the definitions.

If you're going to be a humorist, you need to get the meaning of these styles down. Critic Simon Dentith defines parody as "any cultural practice which provides a relatively polemical allusive imitation of another cultural production or practice."

Huh? Too many big words.

PARODY:
There are a number of definitions:

- A literary or artistic work that imitates the characteristic style of an author or a work for comic effect or ridicule.

- Mimicry of someone's individual manner in a humorous or satirical way.

- Make a spoof of or make fun of.

- A composition that imitates or misrepresents somebody's style, usually in a humorous way.

My favorite definition is that parody is the most aggressive form of comedy writing.

SATIRE:

Some good definitions:

- A literary work in which human vice or folly is attacked through irony, derision, or wit.

- The use of irony, sarcasm, ridicule, or the like in exposing, denouncing, or deriding vice, folly, etc.

- A literary technique of writing or art that principally ridicules its subject (individuals, organizations, governments), often as an intended means of provoking change or preventing it.

Satire is not exclusive to any viewpoint, i.e., there are left-wing satirists who lambaste right-wingers and vice versa.

A "lampoon" is a light, good-humored satire and a written attack ridiculing a person, group, or institution.

Depending on the dictionary you use, "spoof" has pretty much the same definition as lampoon: a gentle satirical imitation; a light parody.

This Is Spinal Tap, labeled by its creators as a mockumentary, is a parody of rock groups. *Airplane* is a parody of '70s disaster films. *The Naked Gun* series is a parody of detective and cop shows. *Scary Movie* was a parody of dead teenager slasher movies. *Don't Be a Menace to South Central While Drinking Your Juice in the Hood* was a parody of overly serious black films. Remember all of the music video parodies by Weird Al Yankovic?

You get it.

What about "farce"? The quick and dirty definition is "a comedy characterized by broad satire and improbable situations."

The more expansive definition of farce: a dramatic genre usually regarded as a subclass of comedy, with emphasis on plot complications and few or no intellectual pretensions. Farce aims to entertain by means of unlikely, extravagant, and improbable situations, disguise and mistaken identity, verbal humor of varying degrees of sophistication, which may include sexual innuendo and word play, and a fast-paced plot whose speed usually increases, culminating in an ending that often involves an elaborate chase scene.

Lots of words, but it's a thorough definition. Think of most of the Farrelly brothers' movies as farces.

Types of farces include screwball comedies and sex comedies. French and Italian filmmakers were great at these.

I'm bringing this up because you need to be knowledgeable about all this stuff. The person who's funny with his friends and family has an easy audience. Once you make a commitment to yourself to try for a career as a comedy writer, it's going to be a tough, uphill climb, so you better know your stuff.

In 2001, after the election of George W. Bush, I co-authored a parody with Sheldon Woodbury called *W. The First 100 Days. A White House Journal*. The idea came from the fact that the first 100 days of every president are considered to be important and indicative of his presidential style. Sheldon and I wrote 100 days' worth of fake journal entries presumably made by Bush.

Like all nonfiction projects, you don't necessarily have to write a complete manuscript. Instead, you do a proposal explaining the nature and scope of the book that contains one or two sample chapters. It's the same with a parody. Sheldon and I wrote 10 pages of fake White House journal entries for Bush. Our agent was able to get us a deal on the strength of those 10 pages. We wrote the rest of the book in three weeks and it was in bookstores within two months.

33

A few years later when conservative columnist Ann Coulter was riding high, I wrote a proposal for a parody on her. She'd just published a book called *How to Talk to a Liberal (If You Must)*. I called mine *How to Have Sex With Ann Coulter (If You Must)*.

My agent liked it and sent it out to editors. Although there was interest, there were no takers. One publisher passed because they published Coulter's books. Another passed because they syndicated her columns. I felt the others passed not because it wasn't good or funny, but because they were afraid to take on Ann Coulter. C'est la vie.

What follows are three of the sample entries that were in the proposal. I did 15 in order to give editors an idea of what the rest of the book would be like, but these will give you a taste of the tone I was shooting for. (Note: As this was written in 2006, some of the content is dated.)

If you have an idea for a parody, you would have to do the same: give editors a sense of what the entire project would be like.

How to Have Sex With
Ann Coulter
(If You Must)

An
Unauthorized,
Autobiographical
Parody

By
D.B. Gilles

(Sample Entry 1)
My Faith

The only area where President Bush and I are on uneasy terms is religion.

He's a Born Again Christian and I'm a Satanist.

I was raised Presbyterian and there was a time back in the day when I did go to church. However, when the Church Elders permitted gays to become ministers I had to leave. I turned to pagan rights and found great comfort in satanic rituals.

This is no doubt why my favorite film of all time is *Rosemary's Baby*, which I saw for the first time in 1968 at the tender age of seven. The reason I was able to get into the movie theater was because I was six feet three even then and looked exactly like Mary of the folk group Peter, Paul, and Mary.

(Sample Entry 2)
Paris Hilton Is Not My Love Child

One of the big lies the left-wing media tried to spread about me in 2003 was that Paris Hilton is my illegitimate daughter.

It's understandable that people might think that Paris *could* be my daughter considering that we're both tall, sexy blondes with fabulous legs and neither one of us has any rear end to speak of.

But come on. No way I would ever have a child without a fine mind. The girl is as dumb as an O. J. Simpson juror.

34

(Sample Entry 3)
My Eating Habits

I know that I'm skinnier than a crack whore on One Hundred Twenty-Fifth Street in Harlem and I'm fine with that. Other than my bingeing and purging during my teen years, food never interested me. It still doesn't.

A typical breakfast for me is half a bowl of Malt-o-Meal Honey Buzzers Cereal and one or two cloves. I usually skip lunch, but once or twice a month I'll chow down on a Funyun Onion Flavored Ring and a Goo Goo Cluster.

Dinner is usually three Trolli Gummy Candy Worms and five Cheese Doodles.

On the fifteenth and thirtieth of every month I eat a bran muffin because I need the fiber.

As I mentioned, the proposal didn't sell, but I had fun writing it and, having written it, I could chalk it up as more experience in writing proposals. I also had a solid writing sample.

The following are examples of parodies that I feel are superb and hilarious. Check them out.

Who Cut the Cheese? — An A-Mazing Parody About Change (and How We Can Get Our Hands on Yours), by Stilton Jarlsberg, poked fun at the serious tome *Who Moved My Cheese?: An Amazing Way to Deal With Change in Your Work and Life*, by Spencer Johnson.

Who Moved My Soap?: The CEO's Guide to Surviving Prison: The Bernie Madoff Edition, by Andy Borowitz.

Chicken Poop for the Soul: Stories to Harden the Heart and Dampen the Spirit, by David Fisher, took aim at the different Chick Soup books.

English as a Second F*cking Language: How to Swear Effectively, Explained in Detail With Numerous Examples Taken From Everyday Life, by Sterling Johnson.

O. J.'s Legal Pad: What Is Really Going On in O. J. Simpson's Mind?, by Henry Beard, was a parody of the fact that during his trial, O. J. Simpson was constantly writing on a yellow notepad.

Governor Arnold: A Photodiary of His First 100 Days in Office, by Andy Borowitz, took aim at the first 100 days of Arnold Schwarzenegger's governorship of California.

writing exercise

Think of three contemporary politicians or bigger-than-life personalities who would be ripe for parody. Using the example of *How to Have Sex With Ann Coulter (If You Must)*, write five sample entries.

Two Catchphrases That Will Be a Part of Your Life From Now on so You Might as Well Know Where They Began

We Are Not Amused & Are We Having Fun Yet?

The royal "we" is the way a person of status, usually a ruler, might refer to himself or herself. Kings and queens are most famous for it, and the royal "we" suggests that the king or queen is something more than a singular person; the ruler speaks both as an individual and as a representative of the people.

Queen Victoria is credited with saying "We are not amused," but after a few Google hits we learn that she may not have actually said it in the royal "we" sense.

According to *The Straight Dope*, her comment is said to have been inspired by the Hon. Alexander Grantham (Alick) Yorke, one of her grooms-in-waiting. Alick's job was to hang around the castle and be funny. As all wits know, however, you're funnier some days than others. On one of Alick's not-so-funny days, some say, he told a risque story to a German guest who laughed loudly, moving the queen to ask that the story be repeated. It was, and she wasn't. Amused, I mean. She was not using the royal "we," though, but rather was speaking for the affronted ladies of the court.

Queen Victoria did not, however, coin the equally popular catchphrase "Are we having fun yet?" That one originated in the American comic strip *Zippy The Pinhead*, created by Bill Griffith. The expression was first used in 1979.

As a comedy writer, you'll find that these two eternal phrases will become a part of your life.

THE MASTERS SPEAK

The satirist shoots to kill while the humorist brings his prey back alive and eventually releases him again for another chance.

— Peter De Vries

If you want to tell people the truth, make them laugh, otherwise they'll kill you.

— Oscar Wilde

I've had great success being a total idiot.

— Jerry Lewis

PART 3

Television: Sketches, Sitcoms, and Late Night

I think that comedy really tells you how it is. The other thing about comedy is that — you don't even know if you're failing in drama, but you do know when you're failing in comedy. When you go to a comedy and you don't hear anybody laughing, you know that you've failed.

— Carl Reiner

A Cautionary Tale
If You Want to Write for Television You'd Better Own a TV

It was a comedy workshop with an emphasis on writing sitcoms. Josh wanted to be a comedy writer. There were several major obstacles in his way:

- He didn't watch television.

- He hadn't watched television on a steady basis since he was 12.

- He hated sitcoms.

- He thought the handful of sketches he'd seen on various sketch shows on TV weren't funny.

- He felt that the only shows worth watching were *I Love Lucy* reruns and Saturday morning cartoons.

- He looked down on people who *did* watch television.

- He didn't own a TV.

I told him he might want to drop the class because he was so ill-prepared. He said why would it matter? How hard could it be to write funny stuff for television?

He was typical of people, students and nonstudents alike, who think writing "funny stuff" for television is easy and doesn't require any skill other than having a sense of humor.

Josh chose not to drop the class. His ignorance, attitude, and arrogance were his downfall. As the semester progressed, Josh lost his smugness as his weekly attempts at writing "funny stuff" crashed and burned. Ultimately he dropped the class.

Something You Should Know That's Not Big Enough to Deserve Its Own Chapter

Finding Your Niche

In the logic of television you are either a writer of comedy or a writer of drama.

You work on a half-hour sitcom/dramedy or an hour-long dramatic show. Seldom does someone who writes comedy make the transition to drama, but it does happen. (To name a few: Alan Ball, creator of *Six Feet Under* and the driving force behind *True Blood*, worked for years on a number of sitcoms. Before joining *The Sopranos* and going on to create *Boardwalk Palace*, Terrence Winter toiled in the sitcom world. David Fury went from writing for *The Jackie Thomas Show* early in his career to *Buffy the Vampire Slayer* to *Lost* to *24*.)

This is called being pigeonholed. It's not necessarily a bad thing. It just helps to narrow the way you are perceived by agents, managers, and people who may hire you.

There is a sublevel of pigeonholing in the world of TV comedy writing. You can either write for a sitcom, sketch shows, or late night television, i.e., comedy news (*The Daily Show*, *The Colbert Report*) or talk (*Letterman*, *Leno*, *Jimmy Kimmel*, *Craig Ferguson*, et al.).

Again, there are some writers who make the transition from one to the other. I worked with Alec Berg and Jeff Schaffer on a sitcom starring Jeff Garlin called *Barkley's Beat* that never made its way to the air. They wrote as a team, having written for shows ranging from *Seinfeld* to *Late Night With Conan O'Brien* to *Curb Your Enthusiasm*.

But the norm is that after finding your niche, you will stay there. To get into a new niche you have to reinvent yourself by

41

writing spec material. So if you're tired of writing sketches or being on staff on a sitcom, write a screenplay. If you've had it with screenplays, write an original pilot. If you want to get away from TV and movies, write a novel or play.

I personally feel it's good for a writer to exercise a different writing muscle and try another genre. Who knows? You may find yourself opening the door to another career.

chapter 6

Writing Sketches

Total absence of humor renders life impossible.

— Colette

Sketches are short and built on a character, situation, or premise. There might be a story or there might not. Just what you need, right, uncertainty? Let me clarify.

A story (be it a sketch, screenplay, sitcom, or novel) has a beginning, a middle, and an end. Some sketches are all story. A character wants something, attempts to get it, encounters obstacles that get in his way, and either gets what he wanted or doesn't. In his journey there must funny lines and actions.

A great *Saturday Night Live* sketch with a strong story starred Jimmy Fallon, Chris Kattan, Jennifer Garner, and Rachel Dratch.

Here's the premise: Jimmy arranged a blind date with twin sisters, Jennifer and Rachel. They arrive at the guys' apartment and we discover that they are conjoined twins attached at the hip. The first surprise is that even though they're twins, they don't look alike. One's hot, the other isn't. And the one who isn't, Rachel Dratch, has bad teeth and a baby's arm sticking out of her head. So the boys argue about who will get which girl. Jimmy ends up getting Jennifer; Chris gets Rachel. As Jimmy and Jennifer start to make out, Chris and Rachel are not hitting it off. Chris is upset because Jimmy is with the more attractive Jennifer. The ultimate payoff is that while Jennifer may be hotter, it's Rachel who has a vagina.

You can Google this and check it out. It never gets old.

Other sketches will be wrapped around a situation, but not necessarily have a story or plot. What's a plot? The placement of incidents.

Another brilliant *SNL* sketch that is more situation than story is *Nicole, the Girl With No Gaydar*. Nicole has no ability to discern if a man is gay. In her sketches she arrives at a place that is obviously filled with nothing but gay men. Only problem is she doesn't realize it, no matter how much evidence there is. There is no conventional story here in that there's no beginning, middle, and ending. The humor comes from the fact that Nicole just doesn't get it. The closest thing to a story comes in the form of a question: Will Nicole realize that the guy she's attracted to is gay? But because she was a recurring character, she couldn't ever come to that conclusion.

Another hilarious sketch featuring Jimmy Fallon also starred Vince Vaughn and Will Ferrell. The premise: Jimmy's character is getting married. He's having drinks with Will and Vince, both older and married for a long time. Jimmy is concerned about certain aspects of marriage, like sex, romance, and in-laws. With every concern he voices, Will and Vince tell him not to worry, marriage is great, sex gets better, in-laws are great, and ultimately they paint such a positive portrait of married life that Jimmy is relieved and happy. He leaves, and then in a serious moment, Vince says, "Should we tell him the truth?" and Will says, "No. Nobody told me."

Perfection.

Keeping with the gay theme, a classic situational sketch that is strong on character comes from *In Living Color: Men on Film*. In this parody of then-popular film critics Siskel and Ebert, David Allen Grier and Damon Wayans portray outrageously effeminate gay film critics, Blaine Edwards and Antoine Merriweather. They review films strictly from a gay point of view. These recurring characters went on to evolve in *Men on Books*, *Men on Television*, *Men on Fitness*, *Men on Vacation*, *Men on Art*, *Men on Football*, and *Men on Men*.

Sketches can also be defined as premise or performance.

How many sketches have you seen that were funny because of the actor? Chances are the sketch itself wasn't very funny on the page, but the actor carried it. This type of sketch is a "performance" sketch. Give Will Ferrell mediocre material and he'll make it sound better and funnier than it really is.

That's not to say that a well-written sketch acted poorly will work. It probably won't in the playing, but in the reading it will.

Writing performance sketches is useless when you're trying to get a job as a sketch writer. You need to write sketches that read funny, because if someone is going to hire you, it will be on the basis of reading your writing samples, not watching them (unless you've made a short comedy video, but more about that later).

A "premise" sketch works because of the words on the page. Someone can read it and laugh. It doesn't matter who plays the parts. The ideal situation is to have a well-written, funny sketch with a great premise and terrific script acted by a top-notch cast. Those are the sketches we remember.

Ultimately, the roadblock to writing good sketches is story. Without one you'll just have characters talking. They might be in a potentially amusing situation, but if all they're doing is talking and the talk isn't based on something that a character wants, the audience will have nothing to wonder about and root for and will lose interest.

That's the plus side of ...

Bits

Another form of sketch is the bit. These don't have a story and barely a situation. Instead, a bit has a vague premise with comic potential or an idea that can be milked for comedy. Late night shows tend to do bits rather than sketches.

Think of "Will It Float?", "Stupid Pet Tricks" and "Hello Deli Games" on Letterman. Leno has "Jaywalking", "The Fine Print," and "Celebrity Jeopardy." From *The Man Show* came "Household Tips From Adult Film Stars," and Conan gave us "The Masturbating Bear" and "Celebrity Secrets."

Take a moment and think of the most memorable sketches and bits you've seen on your favorite sketch shows. Doesn't matter what the show was or when it was on. I loved *Kids in The Hall*, *The State*, *The Man Show*, and *Chappelle's Show*. Lots of people loved *MADtv*, and *Mr. Show* has developed cult status. In the late '90s I also enjoyed *Viva Variety*, a sketch show created by the same people who would go on to star in *Reno 911*. *Saturday Night Live* has taken a beating over its long tenure, much of it unfairly, but the fact is that unlike other sketch shows, it's still here.

45

quick writing assignment

Whichever show or shows may be your pleasure, make a list of your favorite sketches and bits on them. Better yet, rent them on Netflix or see if you can find them through Google and watch them again. But this time watch them with a keen eye.

What was the premise?

Is it premise or performance?

What follows is a list of my 10 favorite sketches from *Saturday Night Live*:

"Nicole, the Girl With No Gaydar"

"Nick Burns, the sarcastic tech support guy"

"The Barry Gibb Talk Show"

"Dick Clark's Receptionist"

"Ed Grimley"

"The Roxbury Guys"

"New Dad Insurance"

"Fernando's Hideaway"

"Debbie Downer"

"Matt Foley, Motivational Speaker"

You've probably seen most of them. If not, try to find them. They are perfection in motion. Not only are they cast brilliantly, but they are hilarious and perfectly structured.

46

Here are some inspired sketches from *In Living Color:*

"Men on Film" (in all its variations)

"Wanda, the Ugliest Woman in the World"

"The Buttmans"

Keenan Ivory Wayans as Arsenio Hall

"Career Aid" (a parody of "We Are the World")

From *MADtv*:

"Cabana Chat"

"Stuart Larkin"

"Dr. Kylie Johnson"

And from *The Man Show*:

"Rest Assured Disposal Service"

"Adam Carolla and His Mother"

"The Man Show Benny Hill Spoof"

Okay. Enough talk. It's time to write a sketch. Here's your first assignment.

sketch writing exercise no. 1

Write a *Saturday Night Live* commercial parody or fake public service announcement. Check out the *SNL Best Commercial Parodies* DVD and see the wide range of possibilities. Aim for four pages or less, but don't stifle your creativity. If it's longer, you can always cut it.

sketch writing for tv vs live performance

You can get away with more when you're not encumbered by network censors. When you're in New York, Los Angeles, or Chicago, check out comedy troupes like Upright Citizens Brigade, The Groundlings, and Second City. That's not to say that you'll have free license to write filthy, vulgar, and tasteless material. It means you can push the envelope more because you won't have a network's "standards and practices" to worry about.

Writing sketches for television limits you. Howard Stern left terrestrial radio because he felt boxed in creatively. If you were to become part of a live sketch or improv group, you could take risks. You would have more freedom to tackle your comedy instincts, but you have to worry about turning off your audience. You can be too esoteric or too highbrow, and it can drive people away.

People watch sketch shows, whether they're on TV or in a theater, to laugh. If you make them feel ignorant, uncool, or uncomfortable, they'll turn on you.

So go easy on religion and sex. Those wacky ideas in the back of your head about Sister Dave the Pedophile Mother Superior and Nigel the Necrophiliac Mortician should probably stay there.

sketch writing exercise no. 2

Write a sketch in which somebody wants something from somebody else, i.e., somebody goes to a FedEx Store and encounters a bipolar clerk; an obnoxious telemarketer is trying to sell meat to a vegetarian who can't say no to anyone; a meek female teenage babysitter must get a foul-mouthed 12-year-old to go to bed.

Writing great sketches is important, but if you can also create a character that can become a recurring character on a sketch show, it's even better.

47

Think of your favorite recurring characters on the sketches you've enjoyed. Somebody had to create them. Maybe it was the actor performing the role. Maybe it was a writer on the show. Maybe it was collaboration between a writer and an actor. But if you can come up with a character that has staying power, it's a huge plus.

Frankly, most sketches are written to stand alone. One performance and out. Even the greatest sketches may only have their four or five minutes of glory and that's fine. But when a character works spectacularly well the first time and there's potential for further installments, that's comedy gold.

sketch writing exercise no. 3

Make a list of your 10 favorite recurring characters on the sketch shows you've watched. Then take a close look at what the character is all about. Is it the actor who makes the sketch work? Is it the dialogue? Is it both?

sketch writing exercise no. 4

Create an original character that could become a recurring character on a sketch show, then write a sketch introducing him or her.

Each week *SNL* has a guest host. The staff writers meet on Monday morning along with the producers and guest host to discuss ideas, concepts, and premises for the upcoming show. Sometimes the guest host has ideas. After some spit-balling the writers go off and put the things they pitched down on paper. The process of writing the script for that week's show, specifically for that week's guest host has begun.

sketch writing exercise no. 5

Pick a celebrity or personality and imagine that he or she is hosting *Saturday Night Live*. Write a sketch for that person. Don't pick someone who has hosted the show. Pick someone who's new on the fame scene.

After completing the above writing exercises, you will have an idea of how difficult it is to write a sketch that works, i.e., that's funny. Coming up with ideas on a consistent basis is hard. Making those ideas have a beginning, middle, and end is hard.

viewing assignment

This will be fun and educational. Check out sketches and bits from the following comedians from the early days of television. They're available on DVD and some sketches via YouTube.

- Milton Berle (*Texaco Star Theater*).

- Sid Caesar (*Your Show of Shows*). And enjoy the work of Imogene Coca, one of the first female sketch stars on television (you may remember her as the grandmother in *National Lampoon's Vacation*).

- George Burns and Gracie Allen (*The Burns and Allen Show*).

- Red Skelton (*The Red Skelton Show*).

- Steve Allen (*The Steve Allen Show*).

- The Smothers Brothers (*The Smothers Brothers Comedy Hour*).

- Carol Burnett (*The Carol Burnett Show*).

10 tips for writing sketches

49

One of the most difficult aspects of sketch writing is ending them. Sometimes even the most perfectly executed sketches peter out at the end. And these are sketches that make it to the air on the various shows.

So when you set out to write sketches, make sure you pay attention to these points:

(1) Don't take too long to introduce the premise. Get to it ASAP and make sure it's clear.

(2) Be sure you have only one premise. Don't introduce a second or third or go off on a tangent, because you will lose the dramatic thrust.

(3) Too many jokes. Back-to-back jokes is overkill. While we're laughing at the first, we may not hear the second and not understand the third because we missed the second.

(4) Too many beats. Sketches need to move quickly and actors need to talk fast.

(5) Let the first drafts of your sketches be longer. Don't stifle your creativity. You can edit them in the rewrites.

(6)   Timing. It's difficult to learn for both an actor and a writer, but once you understand it you'll have a better sense of pacing your jokes. This aspect of sketch writing is best learned when a sketch is on its feet and you can hear actors saying your lines. You'll see what needs tweaking.

(7)   Being politically correct is an important factor. Is what you've written funny or offensive? If you're writing for network television, you need to be aware of boundaries. For live performance less so, but don't be so distasteful that you risk turning away the paying customers.

(8)   Is anything immune from the comic pen? Some hardcore comics and writers feel that nothing is sacred, that anything and everything is up for grabs. This has to be your call.

(9)   How soon is too soon? I know a comedy-writing teacher who had his students write sketches the day after 9/11. For me that's too soon. But I started hearing 9/11 jokes within five months of the attack.

(10) Proofread. Typos, bad grammar, and sloppy punctuation can kill a laugh. And don't try to be too cool, too smug, or too esoteric.

Something You Should Know That Sounds Negative But Is Fact

No News Is Bad News for Comedy

Comedy writers thrive during periods of national instability. If we're perfectly content with our politicians and the world is one big happy place, there's really no point in mocking any of it.

What's bad for the nation is good for the comedy writer. John Edwards, a serious candidate for president of the United States, had a mistress, and if that wasn't bad enough, his wife of many years had cancer, and if that didn't crank up the situation even more, his mistress was pregnant.

Sarah Palin was chosen by John McCain as his vice presidential running mate. She talked funny, she came off as an intellectual lightweight, her unmarried teenage daughter was pregnant, and the child's unemployed father was an Alaskan redneck.

When things go wrong in the world, life is good if you're a comedy writer, especially if you're a staff writer on late night television, where the jokes feed on up-to-the-minute news.

It's not exactly that these writers flip through the news hoping for something horrible to happen, but they're on the lookout for something absurd, illogical, weird, or outrageous enough to pull a few good one-liners, jokes, and sketches from.

So get used to finding material in the agony of others.

51

chapter 7

Bits, Jokes, and Monologues for Late Night TV

The main thing is keeping the main thing the main thing.

— German proverb

Somebody has to write the stuff that talk show hosts say. Why not you?

Watch the credits and see how many writers are on staff. What are the writing jobs on the late night talk and comedy news shows? They can be broken down into the following categories:

- Bit Writer

- Monologue Writer

- Joke Writer

Take *The Late Show With David Letterman*. Somebody has to write Dave's opening monologue, the nightly Top 10 list, and the comical bits they do on the show. As mentioned in the previous chapter, late night shows tend not to do sketches. Writers on late night shows earn their keep by delivering material on a daily basis. If it's five shows a week, that means five times a week the writers must deliver the goods.

A monologue is a set of humorous stories or jokes following one another without a break, told by a comedian or talk show host.

By definition a joke is "a funny story, anecdote, or piece of word-play that gets passed round and repeated."

Depending on the talk show host delivering the monologue, it can contain topical observations of current events in the news that are often political or with a pop culture bent.

The writing staff is there to write all of this material. Check the credits after any of these shows and you'll see a hefty writing staff, including the host of the show. Most hosts do a final pass on the material they'll be doing each evening.

Let's not waste time analyzing this stuff. Just do it.

bit writing exercise no. 1

Come up with three bits: one for Jimmy Kimmel, one for David Letterman, and one for Jimmy Fallon.

After you do that, try this:

bit writing exercise no. 2

Come up with two topics for a David Letterman Top 10 list: one political and one of a general nature. But instead of coming up with 10 for each, come up with 25 for each. Go to CBS.com and check *The Late Show* link to find the most recent examples, as well as the Top 10 archive.

bit writing exercise no. 3

Come up with Seven New Rules a la *Real Time With Bill Maher.* If you're not familiar with his New Rules segment, Google "Bill Maher New Rules."

Let's Talk About Monologues

Every late night talk show starts with a monologue. They're usually topical, dealing with that day's or that week's events both nationally and internationally. Most focus on celebrities and personalities who have done or said something stupid or embarrassing.

Each host has his own style and persona. See how different Letterman is from Leno and how they're both different from Conan O'Brien and how he's different from Craig Ferguson and how Jimmy Kimmel has a unique point of view.

If you're not a regular late night talk show viewer, start. You might want to work for them one day, so you should get to know the style and approach of your potential employer.

The Colbert Report and *The Daily Show with Jon Stewart* are both comedy shows that could be categorized as social satire. Both hosts have entirely different styles. Their opening monologues are less "jokey" than the talk show hosts and more news-oriented.

Jon Stewart's opening monologue is based around one event in the news. He'll talk, maybe cut to a fake correspondent or a newsclip, and talk some more. Somebody has to write that. Because Stewart is a writer himself and the star of the show, he will undoubtedly revise and polish and reshape the material he's given, but before he gets it, someone on the writing staff has to start the process.

writing exercise

Write an opening monologue for Jon Stewart. Don't just watch a few episodes to familiarize yourself with how it works. Study them, analyze them, dissect them moment by moment. Then take your shot. Do the same with Conan O'Brien, David Letterman, Stephen Colbert, and Jimmy Kimmel.

Something You Should Know That's Not Big Enough to Deserve Its Own Chapter

Consistency

It's the ability to be consistent that separates the working comedy writers from the unemployed. If you're lucky enough to get a job on any show that requires fresh batches of material on a daily basis, understand that you have to turn in your work even if you're having a bad day.

There's an old sports maxim: The difference between an amateur and a professional is that the professional plays injured. That applies to comedy writing. Even if you're a laugh whore, you're not going to feel in the mood to be funny every day. An argument with your spouse, girlfriend, boyfriend, or significant other has a way of making your funny bone dry up.

You're sick, depressed, hung over, broke your leg, haven't slept soundly in a month, found out you need $10,000 of dental work, losing your hair, impotent ... whatever ... you have to bite the bullet and get to work.

If you don't, never forget that there are thousands of people who want your job. And if you're not delivering the funny on a consistent basis, you're out.

chapter 8

The Sitcom Spec Script

*You grow up the day you have
your first real laugh — at yourself.*

— Ethel Barrymore

A little background.

Every show on the air is allotted a number of episodes each season, from as few as six up to 22 and often more, depending upon how successful the show is. Being a staff writer means that you'll be assigned at least one episode that you'll write by yourself. You will also participate in the rewriting of each week's script, including your own.

Your real value to a show is how you perform "in the room," as it's referred to in the industry.

The room is the writers' room. This is where the script is revised, reshaped, and rewritten each week by the entire writing staff. Your performance in this venue is more important than your ability to write a script.

Why? Because once a script has been written and approved and is ready to be shot, no matter how good it is, it's going to be rewritten. This is something that new writers find hard to comprehend, especially if important people tell you how great your script is.

Doesn't matter. It *will* be rewritten. Maybe because the star of the show decides his character doesn't have enough laughs or he thinks the subplot is more interesting and he wants it turned into the main plot or one of the producers thinks a story line *he approved* is stupid. There could be a dozen reasons.

It's going to be rewritten by the writing staff in that room. Your value will be in how much you contribute to the end goal of making the script funnier or having more compelling story lines.

If you can do that, you're considered to be "good in the room." If you're a writer who prefers to sit alone in your office at your computer and write and if you're not good at spouting off lines, jokes, and plot twists, you may have a problem. You will be perceived as "*not* good in the room."

Don't concern yourself with that at this point in your sitcom-writing career. You won't know how you'll perform in the writers' room until you get there. You might take naturally to it or you might need some time to adapt.

Constructing the Half-Hour Script

There are five steps in the writing of a half-hour sitcom episode:

- Premise/Story Lines
- Outline/Beat Sheet
- First Draft
- Rewrite
- Polish

There are three kinds of sitcoms:

- Silly but successful: *According to Jim*, *Two and a Half Men*.
- Clever, smart, and well-written: *The Office*, *Big Bang Theory*, *Modern Family*, *Curb Your Enthusiasm*, *Family Guy*, and of course *Seinfeld*.
- Drama/Comedies: *Entourage*, *Sex and the City*, *Hung*, *The Larry Sanders Show*.

Your calling card into the world of television is the spec script. You've probably heard of these. It's simply a script you write for free to show someone (an agent, manager, producer) that you can actually write. But it's important that you choose wisely when deciding which show (and it must be a sitcom that's on the air) to write for.

Always choose a show that's considered to be well-written. Popular spec scripts from the past include *Cheers*, *Frasier*, *Seinfeld*, *Scrubs*, *The Simpsons*, *South*

Park, *Arrested Development*, *The Larry Sanders Show*, *Sex and the City*, and *Taxi*. But you also have to be sure you choose a show that hasn't been spec-scripted into the ground. By that I mean if a show has been on for more than four or five years it's considered "no longer fresh," which ultimately means that if a well-written show is a monster hit, thousands upon thousands of writers will be writing specs for it.

When the American version of *The Office* became the breakout hit of 2005, every ambitious comedy writer in Hollywood was writing specs for it. In my comedy-writing class of 15 people, half would do an *Office* spec. Same with *30 Rock* a couple of years later. Same with *Entourage*, *Sex and the City*, and *Frasier*. But there came a time for each of these shows when, though still huge hits, the common knowledge was that they weren't fresh enough for a writer to spend time writing a spec for. Agents, managers, and producers got tired of reading 25 *Seinfeld* or *Simpsons* scripts every day.

In the best of all possible worlds, with every new season comes at least one breakout comedy. As of this writing, which is in the tail end of the 2010 television season, *Modern Family* is that show.

Guess what? It's the new hot spec. I'm also partial to *The Life and Times of Tim* on HBO.

59

What About Writing an Original Pilot?

If it's going to be the first TV script you'll ever write, I don't advise doing a spec pilot out of the box. They're too difficult and challenging to be your initial effort. Start on a simpler playing field. If you were going to be a playwright, I would have you start by writing a five-page scene, then a 10-minute play, then a 30- to 45-page one act, then a longer one act up to 60 pages, then tackle a full-length play at 80+ pages. Even if you have a great idea, you'd be much wiser to start your journey into the world of sitcom writing by trying your hand at a show already on the air. Preferably, a show you love.

When you write a pilot, besides a compelling premise, you have to create interesting characters and introduce them as you are trying to tell a story. Actually you'll be telling two or three stories. It's difficult introducing characters without tons of exposition, and pilots by necessity have to be filled with exposition.

What's exposition? The giving of information.

Good exposition is when the audience doesn't know it's receiving information. Bad exposition is when a writer overloads his characters with too many details about who they are or what they're doing.

One tried-and-true way of "giving" information is The Ear.

The Ear is the person your main character talks to and listens to. The best friend, roommate, coworker, spouse, brother, sister, significant other, et al.

When you write a script for an existing show, the premise and characters are taken care of for you. You don't have to worry about anything except coming up with a fresh story line. Specifically, two or three story lines, commonly referred to as the A, B, and C stories. Depending on the show there might also be a D Story.

Seinfeld consistently had three story lines, and much of the time they converged at the end. Whether you're familiar with *Seinfeld* or not, episodes air two times a day in most markets, so start studying them.

Right.

Study them.

Don't watch them for amusement. I want you to study, analyze, and dissect them. Count the number of scenes in each act. Figure out how many acts a show has. Some have two; some have three. Watch a few episodes and figure out the average number of scenes an episode has — act by act. Then you'll know how many scenes your spec must have. You can buy scripts for most programs. Check out *SimplyScripts.com* or *planetmegamall.com*.

And your script must have the right amount of scenes. If you've figured out that a typical *Office* script has 15 scenes in Act One and 17 in Act Two, yours should too, give or take.

Also pay close attention to the persona and attitude of each character. Make sure you write lines and jokes that a character would say. Study *Cheers*. Cliff was the bar know-it-all. Carla was the hard-edged barmaid. Sam was the ex-jock womanizer. Diane was the pseudo-intellectual who took herself way too seriously. Those are four beautifully defined characters. To capture their nuances, shadings, and contours means that you must know them inside and out.

You don't want someone reading your spec script saying, "Norm would never say that," or "That doesn't sound like anything Diane would ever say."

Look at *The Office*. Michael is the bumbling boss who says and does things that make people cringe because of their inappropriateness. Kelly is the ditz. Jim is the voice of reason. Andy is the kiss-ass people-pleaser. Angela is the ice queen. Dwight is the backstabbing over-the-top eccentric.

writing exercise

Check every sitcom you watch, both present and past, and you'll see that the central characters are unique unto themselves. They talk and behave in a certain way and that's how you must capture them in your spec script.

Do brief character descriptions of one show's three lead characters.

chapter 9

Writing Your First Spec Script

Comedy is exaggerated realism. It can be stretched to the almost ludicrous, but it must always be believable.

— Paul Lynde

Writing a spec script is hard. Anyone who suggests that it's easy has either never written one, is lying, or is an asshole.

After deciding on the show you're going to write a spec for, the first thing you need to come up with is the premise.

Premise (The A Story)

Basically this is the *TV Guide* description (or log line) of your episode. I love *The Office*, so let's use that as an example.

A Story: Michael decides to become a Scientologist.

B Story: Kevin has a crush on a woman who will only go out with him if he loses weight.

C Story: Angela invites Meredith to join her church choir.

Without much more elaboration you get a sense of where these stories can go.

One further note: When writing your spec, *never* introduce a significant outside character. In the case of the above B story, the woman he has a crush on is only seen once. She would not be considered a significant new character. But if Kevin started to date her and brought her to the office and it was clear that she would appear in future episodes, that's a big no-no.

Writing the Outline/Beat Sheet

The next step is to do an outline or beat sheet, in which you spell out, scene by scene, what's going to happen. These tend not to have dialogue, only description.

Below is a sample outline/beat sheet I wrote for an episode of *The Office* following the above three story lines.

Act One

Scene 1
Michael enters and announces that he's going to become a Scientologist because a new woman he's met is one. Dwight cautions him with a rant about the history of Scientology. The others agree except for Kelly, who asks Michael if he'll introduce her to John Travolta.

Scene 2
At Pam's urging, Jim talks to Michael about the negative image of Scientology. Michael says that any religion with movie stars can't be bad.

Scene 3
In the lunchroom Kevin is eating a salad. Others notice. He admits that he likes a woman who told him she only dates thin guys. Everyone is supportive. Dwight is negative, telling him he doesn't have the discipline. Michael gets involved and says that if he's willing to become a Scientologist for a woman, Kevin should lose weight.

Scene 4 Talking Head
Dwight elaborates on his own discipline when it comes to weight loss. "My great-great uncle Wolfgang Schrute invented the high colonic."

Scene 5
Angela hears Meredith singing in the ladies' room and remarks she would fit in nicely with her church choir, which is looking for a new member. Meredith says she'll show up at a rehearsal. Creed says that he auditioned for *The Gong Show* in the '70s and won.

Scene 6
Jim asks Michael how he found out the new girl was a Scientologist. Michael is vague and says they bumped into each other at the supermarket and it just came up. Jim wonders how Scientology can just come up.

Scene 7 Talking Head
Michael admits to not knowing much about Scientology other than that it made Kirstie Alley gain all that weight and Tom Cruise shrink seven inches.

Scene 8
Dwight catches Kevin eating a piece of celery. He is again negative about Kevin being able to lose the weight. He volunteers to put him on a strict diet and exercise regimen, but demands strict obedience. Kevin agrees.

Scene 9 Talking Head
Kelly thinks it's romantic that Kevin would lose weight for true love.

Scene 10 Talking Head
Kevin admits he's only doing it to get laid.

Scene 11
Meredith shows up at Angela's choir recital and performs well. The choral leader compliments Angela for bringing Meredith in. During rehearsal Angela notices Meredith drinking from a flask and grabbing the butt of the sexy baritone. She warns her to behave.

Scene 12
At Shrute Farm, Kevin is in workout clothes and Dwight is putting him through exercises. He's not doing well.

Scene 13 Talking Head
Kevin wonders if any woman is worth the hell he's going through. He munches on a carrot.

Scene 14
Dwight forces Kevin to drink a disgusting concoction. Kevin resists. Dwight drinks it to show him it's okay and breaks out in a rash.

Scene 15
After checking Wikipedia for Scientology information, Michael is concerned they are aliens and that possibly this woman is in a body disguise and underneath is really a lizard. He discusses this with Andy, Ryan, and Creed.

Scene 16 Talking Head
Creed admits to having had sex with a lizard when he was young and stoned and that it was quite enjoyable.

Scene 17 Talking Head
Michael says he will confront the woman on their first date that night. "I do not wish to go out with a lizard/alien no matter how great her legs are."

Act Two

Scene 18
Meredith shows up drunk at Angela's choir practice and embarrasses her by hitting on the church minister and vomiting onto the organ. Angela is humiliated.

Scene 19
Michael is on his date. He beats around the bush, asking her questions about Scientology. She claims to know very little other than that it's controversial. Michael asks to touch her hand and rubs it a little hard to see if she's a lizard underneath. Finally, the woman has had enough and demands to know what's going on. He tells her that she said she was a Scientologist when they met and now she's denying it and he's afraid she might be an alien and that he's afraid of lizards. She then says that she said she was a science teacher and a biologist. He misunderstood her.

Scene 20
Kevin and Dwight are at the mall about to go into a sporting goods store to buy exercise equipment. Kevin sees the girl who only dates thin guys making out with a fat guy at a food court fast-food shop — someone much heavier than he.

Scene 21
Angela gets into an argument with Meredith because of her obnoxious behavior at choir practice, telling her she is no longer welcome. Meredith says she could care less and that her talent would be wasted. She's going to try out for *American Idol.* "If Susan Boyle can get rich and famous, so can I."

Scene 22
Dwight tells Kevin to confront the woman. Kevin is afraid. Dwight gives him a pep talk and Kevin does so. After telling her off, he takes some food off her plate.

Scene 23 Talking Head
Kevin is munching on junk food and grinning into the camera.

Scene 24
Michael arrives at work looking unhappy. Pam asks how his date went with the Scientologist. He explains that she's not a Scientologist. Everyone is relieved, but Michael says he won't be seeing her again because she's a vegan.

Scene 25 Talking Head
Michael says he can't be with a woman who's a vegan and we realize he thinks a vegan is a virgin.

Scene 26
Meredith and Creed are singing and drinking.

writing exercise

Watch five different sitcoms and write down the A, B, and C story lines for each. And as you watch, study how they are introduced. The A Story comes first, B second, and C third.

The First Draft of Your Spec Script

Once you've done the outline, it's time to tackle the script. Following your outline/ beat sheet, you now write each scene as you described, but this time you put in dialogue and limited action/stage directions.

Always be spare in your stage directions.

Having completed your outline/beat sheet, you have a solid foundation to follow. However, as you write the scenes you only described, you may find that you need to embellish or trim what you wrote. You may realize you don't need a scene or that you need three more. You may find a better way to end Act One or a funnier way of going out on a scene. You may change the ending. You may even lose a subplot and replace it with a stronger one.

That's why it's called a *first* draft.

writing assignment

Track down the pilot episodes of five of your favorite shows just to see how the author(s) introduced characters and plot. You can order them from Netflix. It's even better if you can find the actual scripts.

67

chapter 10

Writing Your First Pilot

Laughter is the sun that drives winter
from the human face.

— Victor Hugo

Historically, pilot deals were gotten without writing much more than a proposal. If you were an established television writer you could sometimes get a deal on the basis of a sentence. There was a defined "pitching season" during which a writer or writing team would pitch an idea to a producer or even directly to a network (usually June to November).

The process was fairly simple. The writer with an idea for a sitcom and the producer he pitched it to would make an appointment with the head of network programming and "pitch" the idea. Working in tandem they would talk it out. The script hadn't been written yet. If a writer had a relationship with a network head, he could often take a meeting and pitch the idea on his own.

My first pilot deal was pitched by myself and two producers from two separate companies who were going to coproduce it. I said very little. They did all the talking.

A year later for my second pilot deal, co-created with Don DeMaio, I had our agent arrange a meeting with a network head that I went to myself without benefit of a producer.

Rarely would a writer actually have written a script. The networks didn't want a finished script. They made their deals based on the pitch. Once the deal was struck they would give notes to the writer, who would then go off and write it.

During the last few years the process has changed. More and more writers, established and brand new, are writing the actual script for their pilots. The logic is that it's easy to say no to an idea or a few paragraphs describing an idea, but if an idea grabs a network head and there's a script ready to be read, you have increased your odds.

There is, however, a process you should follow, even if you've written a pilot. You should have a proposal to go along with your written script.

What follows is a proposal I wrote for a half-hour series I created called *Talented & Gifted*. As you read it pay close attention to how I introduce the premise, ongoing conflict, characters, and sample episodes.

I wrote this not as a wacky half-hour comedy, but rather as a comedy/drama. There are laughs, but the underbelly of the idea is founded in drama.

PROPOSAL

TALENTED & GIFTED

A Half-Hour Series

Created & Written

By

D.B. Gilles

Registered WGA, East

LOG LINE
A gifted but troubled 19-year-old boy is hired as a college professor.

———————

TYLER CANTERBURY has always been the smartest kid in every class he was in. He was smart early on, which is why his parents enrolled him in a Talented and Gifted program at 7.

He graduated from Princeton at 15, Harvard at 19 and published a best-selling novel at 18.

You'd think that Tyler would be on top of the world with a bright future to look forward to.

Not!

Tyler has demons. He has always viewed being talented and gifted as a curse and plays it down at every opportunity. He wishes he were like everybody else: normal and just bright enough to get by. But that's not the case, so inside he's a bundle of anxieties, neuroses, insecurities, occasional delusions, and angst.

He only has one friend, ANNABELLE COLE, 19 and also a prodigy. She plays the cello for the New York Philharmonic. They've been tight since childhood and are each other's confidant. Tyler's self-conscious about his intelligence and feels it has hindered him from having a normal childhood and adolescence. Because he was in college when other kids were in high school his social skills, especially with girls, are virtually non-existent. And he's a virgin, which also hasn't done much for his self-esteem. Unlike Tyler, Annabelle relishes her uniqueness.

On the plus side he has a great relationship with his parents. His father, ANGUS, is a high school dropout and roadie for the heavy metal band Metallica. His mother, JOPLIN, is a freelance cosmetologist for local funeral homes. She was six credits shy of a degree from a community college, but dropped out when Tyler was born.

71

There is also a dark family secret that plagues him. After several episodes it will be introduced into the story line and will play an important role in the development of the series.

Tyler has one way of coping with his problems. He has the ability to lose himself in his imagination. He does so by creating an imaginary alter-ego relationship with his literary hero and inspiration — F. SCOTT FITZGERALD. When Tyler is in a difficult situation, his mind makes F. Scott Fitzgerald appear to offer advice and counsel.

Note: The appearance of F. Scott Fitzgerald is not to be construed as something supernatural, but rather a psychological mind game that Tyler's superior intelligence enables him to create. Tyler talks to Fitzgerald as if he were real, but when he snaps back to reality he knows he only imagined the encounter. Tyler's parents are aware of what Tyler does and they're cool with it.

So the second lead in *Talented & Gifted* is F. Scott Fitzgerald. Not the middle-aged, broken-down version, but the young, witty, and successful 23-year-old model. He talks and dresses as if it were the 1920s.

A weekly surprise in each episode will be the appearance of a famous writer from the past chosen by F. Scott Fitzgerald to teach Tyler a life lesson. It might be a fun casting device to have a well-known actor portray these famous writers.

Tyler gets the teaching job at Hunter College in Manhattan through a friend of his father's who teaches there: ANDREW STACK, 30s, cool and mellow, more like an aging surfer who serves as Tyler's ally. The opportunity comes up when, two days before the fall semester is about to start, another professor is taken ill. Because it's too late to hire anyone of any note, Andrew recommends Tyler to LORRAINE BANKS, the no-nonsense chairwoman of the English department. Reluctantly, under pressure from the dean of the college, she agrees to give Tyler a trial.

Tyler says no when the offer comes, but at the urging of his parents, he takes the job. They want him to do it because he's been in a depressed fog for the last six months. He lives at home, has no social life, and prefers to hang out with his mother (and dad when he's in town). They feel that for his mental and emotional well-being he needs to get out into the world. So he reluctantly takes the job. But he's petrified.

72

However, with the advice of Andrew and, more importantly, F. Scott Fitzgerald, Tyler delivers and he begins his new career as the youngest college professor in the country.

Unlike *Gossip Girl*, which focuses on rich, elitist high school students in Manhattan, *Talented & Gifted* is about smart college kids with the focus on the smartest one among them: Tyler Canterbury.

OTHER CENTRAL CHARACTERS

BLAKE RESHER: 19. From Tyler's past. They were in the same Talented and Gifted program as children. They didn't get along then, but now Blake is a student where Tyler teaches. He appears to be laid-back, but he has a few demons of his own.

HILLARY PENTELLA: 21. A gorgeous student in one of Tyler's classes. He has fallen in love with her, but she's out of his league.

URSULA TWEET: 21. Also in one of Tyler's classes. His nemesis and every teacher's nightmare. She resents having a 19-year-old as a professor and challenges him at every turn.

TAYLOR CANTERBURY: 19. Tyler's twin sister, who will be introduced several episodes into the first season.

RECURRING CHARACTERS

KENNETH OTT: 40. A professor who is jealous of Tyler's early success and shamelessly tries to use him to further his own career.

JAMAL MILES: 30. A professor who shares an office with Tyler. African American.

SIMON WOODS: 50. Also shares an office with Tyler.

———————

Talented & Gifted will be a single-camera show. Sets will be Tyler's residence and at various locations in Manhattan, classrooms, a few faculty offices, and his parents' house.

———————

The pilot script is written. What follows are several sample episodes.

SAMPLE EPISODES

EPISODE 2

(A Story) Tyler is interviewed by a reporter for the college newspaper. When the article appears, things he said were taken out of context and he sounds like a self-involved, pompous jerk. When his students read the article they are standoffish.

(B Story) Tyler and Blake start to hang out. Blake lives in an off-campus apartment. When he finds out Tyler commutes from his parents' house in New Jersey, he suggests that they become roommates. Simultaneously, Annabelle suggests that Tyler move in with her in Brooklyn. Tyler finds himself in an awkward position, especially because Annabelle and Blake dislike each other. A competition for Tyler's friendship begins.

(C Story) F. Scott Fitzgerald introduces Tyler to Jane Austen.

EPISODE 3

(A Story) Tyler's interview is picked up by bloggers and gets nationwide attention, which embarrasses Tyler. He panics and seriously considers quitting. F. Scott Fitzgerald counsels him on how to handle the situation. Tyler discovers that the reporter is Ursula's roommate.

(B Story) Tyler meets the students in the other class he's teaching, The American Novel 1900 to 1950, only to find that half of those signed up have dropped the class in protest. There are just enough students in the class to keep it going.

(C Story) F. Scott Fitzgerald tries to get Tyler and Ernest Hemingway to get along.

EPISODE 4

(A Story) Tyler develops a mad crush on Hillary, who is clearly out of his league. He goes to Andrew for advice on school policy about teacher/student dating and learns that teachers are forbidden to date students. His advice is to wait until the semester is over, then ask her out when she's no longer his student.

(B Story) The class drop-off concerns Chairwoman Banks and she wonders if she's made a mistake in hiring Tyler. Andrew points out that none of the students in his other class dropped. She agrees to be patient. She has another meeting with Hillary and asks her to get to know Tyler better.

(C Story) F. Scott Fitzgerald introduces Tyler to William Faulkner and the three of them go drinking.

EPISODE 5

(A Story) Blake's apartment is very pricey and well-furnished for a 19-year-old. Tyler suspects that Blake is doing something illegal to pay for it. Initially Tyler thinks Blake is dealing drugs, but ultimately finds out that Blake gets top dollar by writing term papers and theses for grad students at colleges throughout Manhattan.

(B Story) Because Hillary is spying on Tyler for Lorraine Banks, she tries to chat him up after classes. He assumes her interest in him is genuine and opens up to her. She reports everything to Lorraine.

(C Story) F. Scott Fitzgerald introduces Tyler to Gertrude Stein.

EPISODE 6

(A Story) Tyler has a victory when his second class gets more students. Word has spread that he's a good teacher. But he has a problem in his first class when Ursula calls him a sexist.

(B Story) Tyler is introduced to Andrew's graduate assistant, an attractive, 25-year-old woman named DEIDRE. She's very kind and respectful of his accomplishments. He begins to suspect that she's having an affair with Andrew (who is married). Tyler has known Andrew and his wife all his life, so he finds the news disturbing and begins to view Andrew in a new light. F. Scott Fitzgerald gives him a life lesson on why married people cheat.

(C Story) F. Scott Fitzgerald introduces Tyler to T. S. Eliot.

EPISODE 7

(A Story) A gorgeous girl Tyler meets through Blake has the hots for him. Blake tells Tyler that she has a thing for guys with high IQs. As the story unfolds Tyler thinks he might finally lose his virginity, but the girl is such a ditz that they have nothing to talk about. Tyler ends up dropping her and remaining a virgin. He realizes he can only be with an intelligent woman.

(B Story) Tyler sees Andrew and Deidre together in an off-campus coffee shop holding hands and kissing. He stares at them a beat too long and Andrew spots him. Later, Andrew and Tyler discuss his relationship with Deidre.

(C Story) F. Scott Fitzgerald introduces Tyler to Agatha Christie.

The information in the proposal combined with the sample episodes will give a network programmer a good idea of the potential of the show.

If all I had was the proposal to try to get a deal, I might have a chance. But if I also have a completed draft of the pilot, my chances are better.

Why?

Because a network programmer can see how I handle dialogue, conflict, character development, and storytelling.

But before I wrote the script I wrote an outline/beat sheet like I did for my *Office* episode.

chapter 11

Turning Your Pilot Idea Into a Script

If you read a lot of books, you're considered
well-read, but if you watch a lot of TV,
you're not considered well-viewed.

— Lily Tomlin

What follows is the outline/beat sheet and script of the pilot episode for *Talented & Gifted* as described in the previous chapter.
Note how specific I tried to make it, but without using dialogue.

OUTLINE

ACT ONE

Scene 1
It's three days before the fall semester is to start. Chairwoman
of the department LORRAINE BANKS meets with two professors,
ANDREW and KENNETH. During the meeting she receives a call
informing her that a key professor in the department has been hit
by a car and will be unable to teach that semester. She turns to
Andrew and Kenneth for help. Andrew suggests someone named
Tyler Canterbury, which results in shock from Lorraine and Andrew.

Scene 2
We meet Tyler and realize that he's only 19 years old, but that he
has graduated from Princeton and Harvard and has published a
best-selling novel. We see him in his bedroom. His mother, JOP-
LIN, wakes him and tells him it's time to get ready for school. He's

nervous, turns to a framed photograph of F. Scott Fitzgerald, and talks to him. After a beat, Fitzgerald comes alive and is sitting on Tyler's bed. We get the feeling this happens often.

Scene 3
Joplin has breakfast waiting. She criticizes his conservative outfit and tells him to dress more casually. She brings up his "imaginary friend" Fitzgerald. Tyler shares his nervousness about teaching a college class. She then gives him a gift: a briefcase for him to use instead of a backpack.

Scene 4
Tyler receives a text from his father, who's out of town. We learn that his dad is a roadie for Metallica.

Scene 5
Joplin drives Tyler to the bus station (they live in New Jersey). They have a heart-to-heart and we learn that he has a sister. They both seem uneasy talking about the sister. We learn that Joplin is a professional cosmetologist and that one of her clients is a funeral home.

Scene 6
Joplin drops Tyler off at the bus station. She puts on a good front, but she's clearly concerned about him.

Scene 7
On the bus into Manhattan Tyler gets a phone call from his best friend, a Chinese American girl named ANNABELLE. She gives him a pep talk. We learn that she is a prodigy on the cello and that she plays with the New York Philharmonic.

Scene 8
Tyler arrives at the campus of Manhattan College. He's nervous and afraid to go inside. F. Scott Fitzgerald appears and gives him a pep talk. It doesn't work. We learn that Tyler is insecure and uncomfortable being so well-educated and successful at the age of 19. Fitzgerald suggests that they have a talk: in Paris.

Scene 9
Tyler and Fitzgerald are at a café in Paris circa 1923 (when Fitzgerald was in his heyday). He continues to build up Tyler's confidence. Then the next thing we know …

Scene 10
They're back in New York on the college campus.

Scene 11
Feeling confident, Tyler enters the building.

Scene 12
He has an awkward scene in an elevator where he innocently checks out the cleavage of a female student. Another female student observes this and sneers at him.

Scene 13
Tyler goes to the office of Andrew (the cool professor from Scene 1) who takes him to meet Lorraine Banks, the chair of the department.

Scene 14
The meeting with Lorraine does not go well. We learn that she's not happy about having a 19-year-old teaching in her department, but that she agreed to it because of pressure from the dean, who thought it would be good publicity for the school. She asks Tyler to leave the office, then tells Andrew that she's giving Tyler a three-week trial period. If he doesn't perform, he'll be out.

ACT TWO

Scene 15
Andrew doesn't tell Tyler about the three-week trial. He tells him to go to the adjunct faculty office to get ready for his class. We learn Tyler will be sharing the office. Andrew says he'll meet him when his class starts in a couple of hours and introduce him.

Scene 16
Tyler is in the adjuncts office when he meets Kenneth (the pompous professor from Scene 1). Kenneth, himself an unsuccessful novelist, immediately tries to use Tyler to help him get an agent. He also tells Tyler that if he has any questions about teaching to ask him. Kenneth leaves. Fitzgerald appears and warns Tyler not to trust Kenneth.

Scene 17
Tyler goes to his first class, still nervous. He calls his friend Annabelle, but gets her voicemail. He then collides with a gorgeous co-ed named HILLARY. She spills her coffee onto his clean white shirt and sport coat. She doesn't realize he's the teacher. He tells her to go into the classroom. He waits for Andrew. Andrew arrives. They step into the classroom.

Scene 18

Andrew introduces Tyler and explains that the professor who would normally teach the class is incapacitated. Tyler will be the new teacher. Upon finding out that he's the famous 19-year-old who wrote the best-selling novel *My Own Private Holocaust* most of the students are in awe. One, however, gives him a hard time. It's the girl who gave him the stink eye in the elevator. Her name is URSULA TWEET. Andrew leaves. Tyler starts to teach. He hesitates. F. Scott Fitzgerald appears and gives him a quick pep talk.

Scene 19

Time cut. Tyler is finishing up. He has won over the class except for Ursula Tweet. They go back and forth. After class he tries to placate her, but she won't cut him a break.

Scene 20

Adjuncts office. Tyler tries to unwind after his class, but he gets an unexpected visitor: BLAKE RESHER, 19. We learn that they knew each other as children in the same Talented and Gifted program. Blake was a bully. Tyler was petrified of him.

Scene 21

We flashback to when they were kids. Blake beats Tyler up.

Scene 22

Back to present. Blake says he has changed. He apologizes to Tyler. We learn that Blake is attending the college and that when he heard about a 19-year-old professor he had to check it out. He wants to hang out. Not really wanting to, but feeling it might be good to have some kind of connection, he agrees. Tyler calls his mom to tell her he'll be catching the afternoon bus so she can pick him up.

Scene 23

Tyler is about to leave. Fitzgerald shows up and with him is Ernest Hemingway (circa 1923). They talk about introducing Tyler to Gertrude Stein, then they disappear.

Scene 24

Lorraine Banks' office. She's talking to someone we don't see at first. She's asking questions about Tyler's performance in the class. A female voice answers and is generally positive. We wonder who it is. We realize it's a spy for Lorraine. We think it's Ursula Tweet. At the end of the scene we realize that it's Hillary, the supposedly ditzy blonde who spilled her coffee on Tyler. Lorraine tells her to keep an eye on Tyler and report back to her.

Scene 25

Tyler leaves the college. Standing outside waiting for him is his father. On a motorcycle. They hug, then jump on the motorcycle and take off. PULLBACK REVEALS that Lorraine is watching from her office window.

Scene 26

Tyler in his room at the end of his first day as a college professor. F. Scott Fitzgerald toasts him.

END OF SHOW

After completing the outline, I wrote the following script. As you read through it you'll see that I took what I wrote in the outline and translated what was described into dialogue and action. Some scenes that were long in the outline are short in the script and vice versa.

See how it turned out.

<u>ACT ONE</u>

EXT. MANHATTAN COLLEGE/NEW YORK CITY — DAY

Friday afternoon, 3 days before the fall semester starts.

INT. LORRAINE BANKS' OFFICE

LORRAINE BANKS, 50, tough, acerbic chairwoman of the English department, stares out the window. She looks upset. Across from her desk sit two professors —

ANDREW STACK, 35, longish hair, the coolest, most popular teacher in the department; and KENNETH OTT, 40, pompous, overeducated snob fussing with his BlackBerry.

> KENNETH
> (without looking up)
> How much longer are we going to wait for him? I could be tweaking my syllabus. I don't know why we're having this meeting anyway.

>   LORRAINE
>   It was your idea, Kenneth.
>
>   ANDREW
>   You called this meeting to discuss the fact
>   that we don't have enough meetings.

Lorraine's phone rings. She answers it.

>   LORRAINE
>   Lorraine Banks ... Sharon, hello ...
>   What?... Oh my God, when?... The important
>   thing is that Peter's all right.... He
>   could've been killed.
>   (cups phone; to Andrew & Kenneth)
>   Peter was hit by a bike messenger an hour
>   ago.
>
>   KENNETH
>   (without looking up)
>   Anything to get out of a meeting.

Andrew stifles a laugh. Lorraine scowls at Kenneth.

>   LORRAINE
>   (into phone)
>   A broken leg, broken arm. Six months he'll
>   be bedridden?... Of course. Thank you for
>   calling. Give my love to Peter.
>   (hangs up)
>   Son of a...! Fall semester starts in two
>   days. Where will I find someone qualified to
>   teach Peter's classes?
>
>   KENNETH
>   (without looking up)
>   Anyone who's any good has already received
>   an appointment. You'll have to choose from
>   the dregs.

                    ANDREW
        What about Victor Artell?

                    KENNETH
                (without looking up)
        Lush.

                    ANDREW
        Walter Pennington?

                    KENNETH
                (without looking up)
        Fired from City College last year. A little
        too touchy-feely with the co-eds.

                    LORRAINE
        This means sorting through those godawful
        resumes I receive every week. There must be
        500.

A beat, then Andrew perks up.

                    ANDREW
        Wait a minute! I might have someone. But
        he's never taught before.

                    LORRAINE
        No. This can't be a learning experience,
        Andrew.

                    ANDREW
        What who I have in mind lacks in teaching
        experience, he more than makes up for in
        credentials. B.A. from Princeton, master's
        from Harvard, wrote an acclaimed best-
        selling novel.

                    LORRAINE
        Get him on the phone.

                          ANDREW
              There might be one little problem.

Lorraine looks at Andrew, waiting.

                          KENNETH
              What was the name of his novel?

                          ANDREW
              My Own Private Holocaust.

Kenneth looks up, his jaw dropping. His BlackBerry
falls to the floor. Lorraine is also stunned.

                          LORRAINE
              Are you talking about Tyler Canterbury?

                          ANDREW
              Yes.

84

                          KENNETH
              I heard it was overrated.
                   (with great sarcasm)
              The inner turmoil of a boy's anguish when he
              learns his beloved great-grandfather was a
              Nazi.

                          LORRAINE
              It made me cry. How do you know him?

                          ANDREW
              When I was in college I was in a rock band
              with his father.

                          LORRAINE
              But Tyler Canterbury is only ...

Off Andrew's awkward expression —

INT. TYLER CANTERBURY'S BEDROOM - DAY

TYLER CANTERBURY, 19, sleeps in his room as the early morning light seeps in. Because his face is half buried in a pillow we don't get a clear view of what he looks like.

The room is filled with hundreds of books ranging from the classics to philosophers and great thinkers to contemporary fiction. It looks more like the library of a middle-aged intellectual.

In a nice frame over his desk is the cover of the aforementioned book he wrote.

Next to it is a framed photograph of F. Scott Fitzgerald as a young man, dressed in 1920s fashion.

The alarm goes off. 7:45 a.m. Tyler sleeps through it.

A beat, then the door opens and a 40-year-old woman, 30 pounds overweight, too much makeup, big hair, too-tight clothes, but sexy, enters.

This is JOPLIN CANTERBURY, Tyler's mom. She has a Southern accent.

                    JOPLIN
          Time to get up, sugar. You don't wanna be
          late the first day of school. Pop-tarts'll
          be ready in 10.

She leaves. Tyler wakes and despite a serious case of bedhead he looks like a typical 19-year-old kid: except for the two-inch-long gray streak in the front of his hair.

He stands and we see that he's skinny and gangly. He stares into the mirror over his dresser.

                    TYLER
          My name is Tyler Canterbury. Welcome to the
          American Short Story: Edgar Allan Poe to F.
          Scott Fitzgerald.
                    (he stops)
          Why am I doing this? I'll be a horrible
          teacher.

He glances at the framed photo of F. Scott Fitzgerald.

                    TYLER (CONT'D)
                    (to the photo)
          Did you ever teach?

Suddenly, time stands still and F. SCOTT FITZGERALD
is no longer in the photo, but now sits on Tyler's
desk chair holding a martini.

86   He's in his mid-20s. His clothing, language, and
     attitude are straight from the 1920s.

                    F.SCOTT FITZGERALD
          Didn't have the temperament for it, kiddo.
          And there wouldn't have been enough money.
          As a wife, Zelda was the cat's pajamas,
          but very high maintenance. You'll be fine in
          the classroom. You're the Real McCoy.

                    TYLER
          I'm tired of being in classrooms.

                    F.SCOTT FITZGERALD
          Better a classroom than to keep hiding from
          the world in your room.

                    TYLER
          I'm not hiding. I'm just ... what's wrong
          with hiding from the world for a while?

> F.SCOTT FITZGERALD
> You've been doing it for six months. You should be traveling, experiencing life, maybe working on losing that virginity?

> TYLER
> Go away.

> F.SCOTT FITZGERALD
> You spend most of your time reading or hanging out with your mother. The last four Saturday nights you went to the mall with her.

> TYLER
> I really don't appreciate being criticized.

> F.SCOTT FITZGERALD
> No one ever does. Get going!

F. Scott Fitzgerald disappears and is again seen in the framed photo.

Tyler takes a beat to adjust to Fitzgerald being back in the photo. We get the idea that this happens on a regular basis. He starts to get dressed.

INT. MODEST SUBURBAN KITCHEN — DAY

Tyler's mom has set a plate with fruit and a Pop-tart at the table. Tyler enters wearing a tweed sport coat, white shirt, and tie. Kind of like the way F. Scott Fitzgerald was dressed.

> JOPLIN
> From the looks of that outfit you've been talking to "F" again.

                    TYLER
Don't call him "F." He hates that.

                    JOPLIN
Honey, if you're gonna have an imaginary
friend I wish he had a better fashion sense.
That outfit might've worked when "Scott"
was around in the 1920s, but don't you think
you're a little overdressed?

                    TYLER
Makes me look older.

                    JOPLIN
You don't need to look older. I thought you
were over that. You know what Doctor
Winchell said: You have the mind of a
brilliant man, the body of a boy and ...

                    TYLER
... the sensitivity of a woman. How could I
forget?

Tyler sits down and starts eating.

                    JOPLIN
And they won't come together until you're
30, maybe 40. You have to learn to
live with it.

                    TYLER
That's the problem. I've been thinking that
this is all a horrible mistake. I'm scared,
Mom.

                    JOPLIN
You were scared at Princeton and Harvard at
first. Compared to bein' a student, bein'
the teacher's gotta be as easy as eatin' a
bowl a gumbo.

                    TYLER
Sitting and listening to someone talk is a
lot easier than being the one doing the
talking. It was horrible enough being the
youngest person in every class I took in
college and grad school. I'll be teaching
two classes. Both to seniors. How horrible
will it be being a teacher younger than
his students?

                    JOPLIN
You're overusing the "H" word again.
          (gently)
It's probably gonna be a little awkward for
the first few classes. Then, once you get
your bearings and a little confidence,
you'll be fine. Remember our family motto.

                    TYLER & JOPLIN
"That which does not kill me, gives me
another day to rock 'n' roll!"

                    JOPLIN
We better go.

                    TYLER
Where's my backpack?

                    JOPLIN
Close your eyes, sweetie.

He closes his eyes. She picks up a beautiful, ex-
pensive, leather briefcase.

                    JOPLIN (CONT'D)
Okay. Open 'em.

Tyler opens his eyes and stares at the briefcase.

> JOPLIN (CONT'D)
> You've outgrown backpacks. I transferred
> everything from your backpack into this.
> This will make you look older. A college
> professor should have a briefcase befitting
> his position.

> TYLER
> Thanks, Mom.

> JOPLIN
> It was your father's idea. You know how
> conservative he is.

QUICK CUT TO:

EXT. TOUR BUS — TRAVELING — DAY

On the side of this top-of-the-line tour bus is
the name of the band: Metallica.

INT. TOUR BUS — DAY

Driving the bus is Tyler's father, ANGUS CANTER-
BURY, 42. Shaved head, tattoos, muscular, pierced
ear. He's a roadie for Metallica.

Angus is texting something.

BACK TO SCENE

> JOPLIN
> Have you checked your messages yet? You
> might find something from him.

Pleased, Tyler reaches for his BlackBerry and
checks his text messages. It's there. He opens
it.

CLOSE ON ANGUS' TEXT:

> *"Make me proud, Ty. No. You've already done
> that.
> Make me prouder."*

Tyler smiles, then punches in a response.

> "Rock on, Pop."

                    JOPLIN (CONT'D)
          Finish eatin'. We gotta go. Bus into
          Manhattan leaves in 15.

EXT. MODEST SUBURBAN HOUSE/NEW JERSEY — DAY

In the driveway we see a pickup truck, a classic
1965 Mustang and a late model Pontiac. The open
garage reveals three motorcycles, one of which is
beautifully tricked out.

INT. JOPLIN'S PICKUP TRUCK — DAY

As she drives, she and Tyler talk. Between them
on the front seat is a small case with a plastic,
see-through top. It contains all kinds of makeup
and beauty aids.

As we'll discover, Joplin is a professional
cosmetician.

                    JOPLIN
          When it's time for lunch don't go off and
          eat by yourself. You need to work on your
          socialization skills. Don't isolate. Doctor
          Winchell says that's when you get in trouble
          and you hide inside that brainy mind of yours.

91

                    TYLER
Sometimes I'd rather not be the brainy one.
It might be fun to be the kid with a high
D, low C average where nothing is expected
of him.

                    JOPLIN
Tyler, you wanted to be a teacher before
you wanted to be a writer. This is gonna be
your chance to see if you can do it. And
you know you will. You've never failed at
anything.

                    TYLER
That's what scares me. I'm overdue. Sometimes
I think that everything good that's going
to happen to me has already happened and
it'll be all downhill from now on. Starting
with me being a horrible teacher.

92

                    JOPLIN
Stop using that word! Nothing horrible has
ever happened to you.

She catches herself for a moment. She looks at
him. He looks at her, as if they're sharing a
dark secret.

                    JOPLIN (CONT'D)
Except for that one time.

                    TYLER
More like three times.
        (beat)
More like five times if we count the night
she ...

                    JOPLIN
Stop! Doctor Winchell says it's not
productive to relive the past.

>   TYLER
>   Sorry, Mom.

They both look straight ahead. There's silence
for a few beats, then —

>   JOPLIN
>   Since you're workin' in Manhattan you
>   should call that nice editor of yours at
>   Random House. They paid you a lot of money
>   for your second book.

>   TYLER
>   That's why I don't want to call her. She e-
>   mails me at least once a week.

>   JOPLIN
>   She's just doin' her job, which is to
>   motivate her authors. You owe her a novel.
>   You have to do the honorable thing.

>   TYLER
>   The honorable thing would be to give back
>   the advance money. I owe her 350 pages. So
>   far I've written 28.

>   JOPLIN
>   (cheerfully)
>   That means only 322
>   pages to go.

A moment of silence, then...

>   TYLER
>   Do you always have to be so optimistic?
>   (beat)
>   How many bodies will you be working on
>   today?

                    JOPLIN
        Three.

EXT. NEW JERSEY BUS STATION — DAY

Tyler's mom pulls up to the bus depot. As Tyler
gets out of the car she leans over and gives him
a kiss on the cheek.

                    JOPLIN
        You're gonna do just fine, sugar.

Tyler's mom watches him walk away with pride, but'
there's also concern on her face.

INT. TRAILWAYS BUS — DAY

Tyler sits on the commuter bus, his laptop before
him, making notes for his first lecture. He also
holds the syllabus of one of the courses he'll be
teaching (created by the professor he's replacing).

After a beat, his BlackBerry rings. He answers it.

                    TYLER
                (into phone)
        Hey, Annabelle!

INTERCUT

INT. REHEARSAL AREA — DAY

ANNABELLE CHENG, 18, Chinese American unsmiling,
overly serious, has a don't-mess-with-me look.
Barely five feet tall.

                    ANNABELLE
        Figured I'd touch base because I know your
        self-loathing has undoubtedly kicked in by
        now, which means the evil spirit who lives
        in your soul won't be far behind.

94

                    TYLER
I'm fine. My class isn't 'til two. The other one isn't until Wednesday. I'm trying
to figure out what my first lecture will be.
They e-mailed me the guy I'm replacing's
syllabus. I was thinking of following it.

                    ANNABELLE
Do your own, dimwit. Don't think of yourself as a replacement. Blow the old guy out
of the water. Drive a stake in his heart
and take over his turf. This is just the
beginning. Get your goals in order. You're
gonna be the youngest person to ever get
tenure at an American university.

                    TYLER
Annabelle, you're the megalomaniac, not me.
I don't want to be the youngest anything
ever again.   95

                    ANNABELLE
You and I have been given gifts. We had
lousy childhoods, no friends except for
each other and we can't get laid. I have to
go. Good luck, stupid.

                    TYLER
Thanks, moron.

They both smile as they hang up.

PULL BACK ON ANNABELLE TO REVEAL that she holds a
cello. We realize that she is a cellist with the
New York Philharmonic.

EXT. FUNERAL HOME — DAY

Joplin pulls into the parking lot.

INT. WORK ROOM/FUNERAL HOME — DAY

"Sweet Home Alabama" plays in the background as
Joplin applies makeup to the corpse of a woman in
her 70s.

EXT. MANHATTAN COLLEGE CAMPUS — DAY

Tyler approaches a building with an imposing
sign:

SCHOOL OF ARTS & SCIENCES

He stops and checks out the students heading to
classes: all different types from 18 to 22. They
all look intimidating. Suddenly, all the students
stop what they're doing and stare at Tyler.

Then, a la *Night of the Living Dead*, they start
marching toward him. Tyler panics, starts to back
away, but he's surrounded by more zombie students.

96

                    F.SCOTT FITZGERALD (V.O.)
          What are you waiting for, kiddo?

ANGLE ON

F. Scott Fitzgerald sitting on a bench checking
out the girls. He waves Tyler over. Suddenly, the
zombie students are gone and the students continue with their normal business.

                    TYLER
          The students here are going to eat me
          alive. I can't do this.

                    F.SCOTT FITZGERALD
          Are you in need of a pep talk?

                    TYLER
     I'm feeling queasy. I should probably eat
     something.

                    F.SCOTT FITZGERALD
     Then let's go have some French cheese.

                    TYLER
     Will we have time?

                    F.SCOTT FITZGERALD
     You slay me. There's always time to go to
     Paris.

He extends his hand. Tyler takes it. After a
beat, both have disappeared.

EXT. AERIAL SHOT OF PARIS — DAY

The Eiffel Tower, Arc de Triomphe, the Seine and   97
as we come down to Avenue des Champs-Élysées we
see automobiles and trolleys circa the 1920s.

EXT. PARIS/AN OUTDOOR CAFE — DAY

It's 1923 in Paris. Tyler and Fitzgerald sit
at an outdoor table eating a plate of cheese.
Fitzgerald sips a glass of wine, Tyler a Coca-
Cola.

Other customers and passersby are all dressed in
the fashion of the time.

                    F.SCOTT FITZGERALD
     I published my first novel when I was 23. I
     was a boy wonder too. It changes everything
     ... and not all for the better. But you al-
     ready know that.

A waiter passes by. Fitzgerald points to his empty
wine glass. The waiter nods.

> F.SCOTT FITZGERALD (CONT'D)
> Emily Dickinson summed it up nicely.
> "Success is held dearest by those who never
> achieve it." Have I introduced her to you
> yet?

> TYLER
> No.

> F.SCOTT FITZGERALD
> You'd love her. A bit shy. The "poet's
> mentality" and all that. But once she's had
> a spot of brandy, she loosens up.

The waiter returns with a fresh glass of wine.

> F.SCOTT FITZGERALD (CONT'D)
> Merci. I used to wonder how things would
> have turned out for me if had a chance to
> live a more normal life before fame came
> knocking.

> TYLER
> Normal is all I ever wanted.

> F.SCOTT FITZGERALD
> Normal means being ordinary. Not unique.
> You haven't had the chance to experience
> the rewards that come with being extraordinary.
> Once you have, "normal" is a condition you
> will avoid at all costs.
> (beat, suddenly serious)
> Normal becomes your enemy. When I died I
> was living a normal life. Hand to mouth.
> Struggling to get by. C'est la vie. So I
> thank you for bringing me back to life as a
> figment of your imagination.
> (checks his watch)
> Drink up. You have a class to teach.

98

They disappear.

After a beat, Tyler stands alone in front of
the Manhattan College entrance. He takes a deep
breath and enters the building.

INT. HALLWAY — DAY

Tyler walks toward an elevator filled with students, mostly female, chatting animatedly. He
steps inside.

INT. ELEVATOR — DAY

It's a tight squeeze. Two girls wear tight tank
tops with cleavage visible.

Tyler can't help but stare at the almost uncovered
breasts of a sexy blonde. As he does so he notices
a plain, mean-faced girl watching him stare at
the blonde's chest. She gives him the stink eye.
His face turns red as he looks away.

INT. CREATIVE WRITING DEPARTMENT — DAY

Tyler heads down the hallway passing offices of a
few other faculty members sitting at their desks,
preparing for the first day of classes.

Tyler comes to Andrew's office. The door is open.
He knocks politely.

INT. ANDREW'S OFFICE — DAY

It's not large, but it has a window and it's
decorated kind of funky. Many books, framed book
jackets of novels, stacks of student manuscripts.

CLOSE ON A PLAQUE proclaiming Andrew as Distinguished
Teacher of the year.

                              ANDREW
                    Tyler! Come in.

          Andrew stands and gives Tyler a hug. Tyler is relaxed.

                              ANDREW (CONT'D)
                    I can't tell you how grateful I am that you
                    agreed to do this.

                              TYLER
                    I hope you don't come to regret it.

                              ANDREW
                    I'm not worried. You'll do fine.
                         (beat)
                    But not today. Twenty students will be
                    showing up expecting to have Peter Fleming
                    as their professor. I'm going to be there
                    to explain the situation and introduce you
100   to the class. Wouldn't surprise me if half
                    of them have read your book, so there'll be
                    a recognition factor. And they'll like the
                    fact that you're the same age.

                              TYLER
                    They're all sophomores?

                              ANDREW
                    Seniors.

                              TYLER
                    Then they're two years older than me.

                              ANDREW
                    Tyler, you're an old soul. You wrote a
                    best-seller. Our students all want to be
                    novelists. You've already accomplished what
                    they're only dreaming about. They want to
                    be you!
                         (beat)
                    Meanwhile, we need to get you a photo ID and
                    I want you to meet your new boss.

INT. CAMPUS ID OFFICE — DAY

Tyler gets his picture taken for his photo ID.
The camera flashes. It's not a flattering picture.

INT. LORRAINE BANKS' OFFICE — DAY

In Lorraine's office. Andrew is introducing Tyler
to Lorraine. They shake hands. Lorraine smiles
graciously. Tyler smiles nervously. We don't hear
what's being said, then —

                    LORRAINE
          Tyler, Andrew believes you can do this. I
          want to believe you can do this. I have one
          question. Do you believe you can be an
          effective teacher?

Tyler hesitates and looks panicked. He can't
speak.   101

F. Scott Fitzgerald suddenly appears behind Lorraine.
He's nodding his head up and down.

                    F.SCOTT FITZGERALD
          Just say yes.

                    TYLER
               (to Fitzgerald)
          But I don't think I can.

                    LORRAINE
          Tyler, did you hear me?

                    F.SCOTT FITZGERALD
          Say yes!

                    TYLER
               (to Lorraine)
          Uh ... yes.

> LORRAINE
> Tyler, would you give Andrew and me a
> moment?

Tyler nods okay, then leaves. Lorraine waits for
him to be out of the office before speaking, then —

> LORRAINE (CONT'D)
> My God, he looks even younger than 19. How
> screwed up is he by his early success?

> ANDREW
> He's uncomfortable with it.

> LORRAINE
> I'm uncomfortable with him being in my
> department. The only reason he's here is
> because I'm under pressure from the dean.
> I told him about Tyler, assuming he would
> think it's preposterous, but he loved the
> idea. Enrollment's been down the last two
> years. He felt having a 19-year-old
> professor would be good publicity for the
> college.
>   (beat)
> I convinced the dean to give Tyler a trial
> period of three weeks.

> ANDREW
> That's not nearly enough time.

> LORRAINE
> That kid has no real life experience. I
> couldn't find anyone else with two days' no-
> tice. There were no options.

> ANDREW
> It takes an experienced teacher three weeks
> to get his momentum going.

                    LORRAINE
The students will be the gauge. Word
spreads quickly when a teacher isn't
cutting it. I asked someone in his class to
report back to me on his performance.

                    ANDREW
Give him a break.

                    LORRAINE
I did. I hired him against my better
judgment. If he works out, great. If he
crashes and burns I don't want to be part
of the wreckage. Three weeks. That way
there'll still be time to bring in someone
else.

                    ANDREW
If necessary.

                    LORRAINE
If necessary.

Off Andrew's disappointed face.

                    END OF ACT ONE

                    ACT TWO

INT. HALLWAY — DAY — IMMEDIATELY FOLLOWING

Andrew comes out of Lorraine's office. With Tyler
at his side they walk. Because of the conversation he just had with Lorraine, Andrew is less
upbeat.

> ANDREW
> Listen, I have a class in a few minutes.
> I'll meet you in front of your classroom
> at two so I can introduce you. Meanwhile,
> if you need some privacy to go over your
> notes, go to the adjuncts office.

Tyler and Andrew walk.

> ANDREW (CONT'D)
> Because you're an adjunct you'll be sharing
> an office.

They turn a corner.

> ANDREW (CONT'D)
> Because of different teaching schedules,
> you'll hardly ever see some of the people
> who use the office.

104

They stop in front of the adjuncts office. The
door is open.

> ANDREW (CONT'D)
> Here we are. You can use the empty desk.
> See you at two. Room 426.

Andrew walks off. Tyler enters the adjuncts office.

INT. ADJUNCTS OFFICE — DAY

A cramped space with four desks crammed together,
a bookcase, and an old file cabinet. One desk is
empty. The other three have bare-minimum stuff on
them: old computers, phones, calendars, pencil
caddies. Nothing fancy.

Tyler steps inside. Sets his briefcase on the
empty desk. He removes his lecture notes from his
briefcase and sets them on his desk. After a few
seconds ...

                    MALE VOICE (O.S.)
          What do you think you're doing in here?

Tyler spins around and we see that the voice be-
longs to Kenneth Ott, who we met earlier.

Kenneth suddenly realizes who Tyler is. He stiffens
up.

                    KENNETH
          Oh. It's you.

                    TYLER
          Excuse me.

                    KENNETH
          Tyler Canterbury.

He extends his hand. Tyler shakes it.

                    KENNETH (CONT'D)
          Kenneth Ott. How did you manage to get your
          short story published in *The New Yorker*?

                    TYLER
          They asked me to write one for them.

                    KENNETH
          I see. I understand you're a Harvard man.
          What fraternity?

                    TYLER
          None. I was 16. They were worried about
          lawsuits and child abuse issues.

                    KENNETH
          I understand this is your first time teaching.
          Any questions in dealing with the godless
          bastards who study here, feel free to pick
          my brain.

105

>   TYLER
> Uh, okay.

Kenneth starts to leave, then stops.

>   KENNETH
> One more thing: Do you have access to the
> fiction editor of *The New Yorker*?

>   TYLER
> Yes.

>   KENNETH
> I'm putting the finishing touches on a short
> story. Unfortunately, I don't have a way to
> reach the man.

>   TYLER
> I could give you his e-mail and you can
> contact him directly.

106

>   KENNETH
>   (almost childlike)
> You have his e-mail?

>   TYLER
> The one at work and the one at home.

>   KENNETH
> Jot them down when you get a chance. This
> is my desk.

Kenneth reaches for a folder and a book.

>   KENNETH (CONT'D)
> I'm off to my class. Pleasure to meet you,
> Tyler. One tip: Don't make any eye contact
> with your students and never eat any food
> they might give you.

Tyler nods, then Kenneth leaves.

Suddenly, F. Scott Fitzgerald appears.

                  F.SCOTT FITZGERALD
      Don't trust him. He wants to use you. I had
      to learn the hard way. Fortunately, I had
      my wife to look out for me. You're much
      too young to get married, but you'll need
      a woman of Zelda's caliber to field off the
      locusts.

                  TYLER
      My friend Annabelle is very good at that.

                  F.SCOTT FITZGERALD
      When in doubt, check with her.

Fitzgerald waves good-bye and disappears.

107

INT. ARTS & SCIENCE BUILDING HALLWAY — DAY

Students head to and from classes. Tyler approaches Room 426. Andrew isn't there to introduce him. Several students pass by him and enter the classroom.

Tyler grabs his Blackberry and calls Annabelle. He gets her voicemail.

                 ANNABELLE'S VOICEMAIL
      Only two people have this number, so unless
      you're Tyler, my shrink or you have
      unbelievably good news ... go F yourself.
      Have a nice day.
          (BEEP)

                  TYLER
      It's me. I'm about to go into my class
      and I'm starting to panic. I needed an
      Annabelle fix. Later.

He peers inside the classroom and sees 20 students sitting in their seats staring at their notebooks or straight ahead.

A gorgeous girl, HILLARY PENTELLA, 21, rushes toward Tyler carrying an open-topped cup of coffee. She wears a short skirt.

They collide and her coffee splashes onto Tyler's shirt. It's a mess.

                    HILLARY
               (ditsy, over the top)
          Oh my God! I'm so sorry. I thought I was
     late for class. I hate being late the first day. I
     have this thing about being on time.

Hillary reaches into her bag and removes several tissues. She tries to soak up the coffee. She's rubbing Tyler's stomach and chest area aggressively.

                    HILLARY (CONT'D)
          I'm such a klutz.

                    TYLER
          It's okay. These things happen.

Tyler looks up and sees Andrew approaching.

                    TYLER (CONT'D)
               (to Hillary)
          You should probably go into the classroom.

                    HILLARY
          I'll pay for the dry cleaning.

                    TYLER
          It's okay.

Hillary gives him a friendly smile and goes into the classroom. Tyler is in love.

Andrew comes up to him. Notices the coffee stain.

                    ANDREW
          Sorry I'm late. We should go inside.

                    TYLER
               (re: coffee stain)
          I can't go in looking like this. They'll
          laugh at me.

                    ANDREW
          This is actually good. It'll humanize you.
          I left something for you on your desk.
          Let's go.

They step into the classroom.   109

INT. TYLER'S CLASSROOM — DAY

Tyler follows Andrew to the front of the class.
Andrew reeks of gravitas while Tyler slinks in
shoulders dropping and looking frightened.

The kids can't help but notice the coffee stains
on his shirt and jacket. A few smirk and giggle.

                    ANDREW
          Good afternoon. I have some unfortunate
          news. Due to a serious accident on Friday
          Professor Fleming is unable to teach this
          class.

There are looks of surprise/concern/etc. from the
students.

                    ANDREW (CONT'D)
          Fortunately he's okay, but he'll be out for
          the semester. The good news is that we've
          found a replacement. You may not know this
          young man by sight, but I'm sure you know
          his name. The author of the best-selling
          novel *My Own Private Holocaust* ... Tyler
          Canterbury.

There are different looks now. Several of the
guys straighten up in their seats.... A couple of
girls light up. Smiles from the students who know
the book ... curiosity from others.

Hillary Pentella sits up, even more embarrassed
that she spilled coffee on Tyler.

ANGLE ON one girl who smiles broadly, reaches
into her bag, and removes a copy of Tyler's
110   novel. She raises her hand.

                    ANDREW (CONT'D)
          Yes?

                    SMILING GIRL
               (to Tyler)
          I loved your book. Will you autograph my
          copy?

                    TYLER
          Okay.

A gay kid raises his hand.

                    GAY KID
          You really reached out to gay teens through
          your protagonist's best friend, Adam. I
          totally identified with Adam. You got into
          my soul.

                        TYLER
        Thank you.

Then an unseen female voice shouts out ...

                        FEMALE VOICE
                (accusatory)
        What are your qualifications to teach this
        course?

Tyler looks to see who asked the question and is
stunned to see someone we've met before —

The mean-faced girl in the elevator who glared at
Tyler.

Her name is URSULA TWEET, 21, self-assured,
entitled, and with a look of perpetual anger.

                        ANDREW
        That's irrelevant. He was appointed to the
        position by the chair.

                        URSULA
        The hundred thousand dollar student loan
        I'll have to start paying off next year
        says that it is relevant. I waited three
        semesters to study with Professor Fleming,
        not with someone who published his thesis
        as a novel and who may very well be a one-
        shot wonder.

The other students look at her, as does Tyler.
Even Andrew seems at a loss as to what to say.

F. Scott Fitzgerald appears at the back of the
classroom.

                        F.SCOTT FITZGERALD
        Remember what your therapist said.

                    TYLER
          What are you doing here?

                    F.SCOTT FITZGERALD
          Watching your back. Doctor Winchell said
          that your achievements have been unhealthy
          for your psyche. You have an overdeveloped
          passivity and a latent aversion to conflict.
          When a difficult situation arises you must
          rely on the old T and M. Truth ...

                    TYLER
          ... and modesty. I get it. Go away. You're
          breaking my concentration.

     F. Scott Fitzgerald disappears.

     BACK TO SCENE

112   TYLER (CONT'D)
          What's your name?

                    URSULA
          Ursula Tweet.

                    TYLER
          That's a very cool name. It's a writer's
          name.

                    URSULA
          I hate it.

                    TYLER
          I hate mine too. Tyler Canterbury sounds
          more like a NASCAR driver.

     The rest of the class laughs. Ursula doesn't.

                    TYLER (CONT'D)
          Yeah. Uh, Ursula, you're right. I did
          publish my thesis. I was very lucky that my
          professor had connections at Random House
          and that I had a great editor.

                    URSULA
           Are you saying that she was the driving
           force behind your novel and not you? That
           your reputation is based on the work of
           someone else?

                    TYLER
           It's very possible.

The students react to his comment with surprise
at his honesty.

                    TYLER (CONT'D)
          And if the writer's block I've had since my   113
          book came out is any indication, there's
          a good chance I'll be a one-hit wonder. I
          hope not.
                (beat)
          As for your concern that I'll be able to
          teach? I can tell you right now that I
          won't be anywhere near as good as
          Professor Fleming. But I studied with some
          great teachers at Princeton and Harvard ...
          and I took lots of notes ...

The class laughs except for Ursula.

                    TYLER (CONT'D)
           All I can say is that if you decide to drop
           the course, you won't hurt my feelings.

                    URSULA
           I can't drop the course even if I wanted
           to. Everything else is closed.

                    TYLER
              (friendly)
          Then we're stuck with each other.

The students laugh at his remark ... except for
Ursula.

                    URSULA
          No. I'm stuck with you!

Ursula has managed to cause a dead silence in the
room.

                    ANDREW
          Okay. If there are no more questions ...
          I'll leave you in Tyler's capable hands.
              (leans into Tyler)
          Welcome to the dark side of education.

114   Andrew leaves.

                    TYLER
          Okay then.

Hillary, who's wearing a short skirt, crosses her
legs, revealing plenty of thigh.

Tyler can't help but stare at her legs.

ANGLE ON

F. Scott Fitzgerald who sits at the desk next to
Hillary checking her out.

                    F.SCOTT FITZGERALD
              (re: Hillary)
          If she's not the bee's knees, I don't know
          what is.

                    TYLER
          You're breaking my momentum.

                 F.SCOTT FITZGERALD
          Remember: You won't be able to date her
          or any of these skirts? Colleges frown on
          teacher/student affairs these days? When I
          was at Princeton it was considered a perk.

                    TYLER
          Thanks for the tip. Now if you don't mind,
          I'd like to start my class.

                 F.SCOTT FITZGERALD
          Don't take any wooden nickels!

F. Scott Fitzgerald takes one final look at Hillary and disappears.

Tyler settles in at the podium, takes out his   115
lecture notes and looks at the class.

                    TYLER
          Welcome to the American Short Story: Edgar
          Allan Poe ... to F. Scott Fitzgerald.

TIME CUT

One hour later. Tyler has written words like
theme, subplots, etc. on the whiteboard. He looks
more relaxed.

                    TYLER
          Has anyone ever visited the grave of an
          author you like?

The students react to the question with confusion.
One girl raises her hand.

>   GIRL
>   Does Jim Morrison count? I saw his grave at
>   a cemetery in Paris.
>
>   TYLER
>   Père Lachaise. Many French writers are
>   buried there. I like to visit the graves of
>   my favorite authors.

CLOSE ON Ursula who rolls her eyes.

>   TYLER (CONT'D)
>   My father is a roadie for Metallica. When
>   I was younger I traveled with him. To pass
>   the time he liked to visit old cemeteries and
>   look for famous people's graves. I thought
>   it would be cool to visit the final resting
>   place of writers. Helped me get in touch
>   with their spirits.

116

CLOSE ON Ursula.

>   URSULA
>   Give me a break.
>
>   TYLER
>   Pardon?
>
>   URSULA
>   Nothing.

TIME CUT

Most of the students look as if they're liking
the class. There are a few bored faces, including
Ursula's.

>   TYLER
>   Because my being hired happened so fast,
>   I haven't finalized the syllabus, but I'll
>   have it for you next week.

He looks at the clock at the back of the room.

                      TYLER (CONT'D)
So unless there are any questions, that'll
be it for today.

                      FEMALE STUDENT #2
What should we call you? Professor or Mr.
Canterberry?

                      TYLER
Call me Tyler. Okay. I'll see you next
week.

The students disperse. Hillary approaches Tyler.

                      HILLARY
Will the fact that I spilled coffee on you
affect my grade?

                      TYLER
No.

                      HILLARY
Thank you. I'm Hillary Pentella.

She extends her hand. Tyler shakes it. He holds
on to it for a beat too long.

                      TYLER
Nice to meet you.

                      HILLARY
I didn't read your book, but I'm going
to buy a copy. I think it's so cool that
you're our teacher instead of some old guy.

                      TYLER
Thanks.

Hillary leaves. There are still a few students in
the class. One of them is Ursula Tweet. She heads
for the door.

                    TYLER (CONT'D)
          Ursula?

                    URSULA
          Yes?

                    TYLER
          We got off to a bad start. You sounded
          angry.

                    URSULA
          I always sound like I'm angry. I wanted to
          study with Peter Fleming, not somebody two
          years younger than me.

118

                    TYLER
          I understand. I'll do my best to live up to
          your expectations.

                    URSULA
          I don't have any. Just don't bore me.

She leaves. Tyler shakes his head back and forth.

INT. ADJUNCTS OFFICE — DAY

Tyler enters. The office is empty. He goes to his
desk and notices a gift-wrapped present in the
middle — the gift that Andrew referred to. He
opens it and removes an 8 x 12 frame and looks at
what's in it. He smiles.

There's a knock on the door. Tyler looks up to
see a male student, 19, long hair, laid-back,
radiates the bad boy image.

This is BLAKE RESHER.

> BLAKE
> Hey brainiac!

Tyler looks up, startled, as if the name resonates. He looks closely at Blake, then his face
turns red as he sits upright.

FLASHBACK TO 9 YEARS AGO

A playground where 10-year-old Blake is picking
on 10-year-old Tyler. Pushing him, punching him,
and knocking him down.
Tyler doesn't fight back.

> 10-YEAR-OLD BLAKE
> Stupid freakin' brainiac! You think you're
> smarter than everybody. You're not smart
> enough to fight me, you freakin' brainiac.

119

Tyler curls up into a ball as Blake continues
pounding him.

BACK TO SCENE

> BLAKE
> I heard you were teaching here. Very cool.
> We were in the same Talented and Gifted
> program. We both had IQs of 168. I used to
> pick on you.

> TYLER
> Blake Resher.

> BLAKE
> I had real anger management issues back
> then. Lots of insecurity despite my so-
> called intelligence. They kicked me out
> when I was 11. I was a real jerk. I blame
> the Ritalin. I hope you won't hold it
> against me.

He walks in uninvited and sits down.

                    TYLER
          Uh, have a seat.

                    BLAKE
          I came out of a class and I hear about this
          19-year-old professor. I think someone's
          yanking my chain. Then I find out it's you.

                    TYLER
          So you're a student here.

                    BLAKE
          Sophomore. I had to come by and say hey.
          Weird that we're both here. You still in
          touch with that Chinese chick who was in
          school with us?

                    TYLER
          Annabelle. She's my best friend.

                    BLAKE
          Yeah. She would report me every time I beat
          you up. I read your novel. I'm jealous. In
          a good way.

                    TYLER
          Thanks.

                    BLAKE
          Everybody here will be jealous including
          most of the teachers. Guess you really were
          talented and gifted. I crashed and burned
          at 13. My parents put me into private
          school, military school, then rehab. I've
          had years of therapy. But it's all good
          now.
               (beat)
          Listen, I know it's been nine years and
          you're a professor ...

                    TYLER
     I'm not really a professor. I'm technically
     just a teacher.

                    BLAKE
     Whatever. If you feel like it, maybe we
     could get coffee sometime. But if you still
     hate me for the way I treated you when we
     were 10, I'll keep away.

Tyler hesitates for a beat.

                    TYLER
     We were kids. I teach on Mondays and
     Wednesdays.

                    BLAKE
     I'm here then too. My e-mail's easy to
     remember. Blake@mac.com. Shoot me an e-mail
     with your contact info.   121

                    TYLER
          Okay.

Blake fist-bumps Tyler, then leaves. Tyler watches
him go, not quire sure what to make of him.
He pulls out his BlackBerry, punches in a number.

INT. FUNERAL HOME — DAY

Tyler's mom is doing the makeup on another female
corpse when her cell phone rings. She sees that
it's Tyler.

                    JOPLIN
          Hi, sugar. How'd it go?

                    TYLER
     It wasn't horrible. Could've been a lot
     worse. A lot worse.

                    JOPLIN
        That means it went very well.

                    TYLER
        I'm about to leave. I'll call you when the
        bus arrives?

                    JOPLIN
                (she smiles)
        Yeah. See ya later, professor.

They both hang up, then ...

ANGLE ON

F. Scott Fitzgerald sitting on one of the other
desks. Sitting next to him is ERNEST HEMINGWAY
(in his mid-20s) looking macho and unfriendly.

122

                    TYLER
        What's he doing here? You know I don't like
        his novels. It's only fun meeting authors I
        like.

                ERNEST HEMINGWAY
        Why don't you like my novels?
                (re: Fitzgerald)
        I had more best-sellers than him.

                F.SCOTT FITZGERALD
                (to Tyler)
        C'mon, kiddo, he's one of us. Published his
        first novel at 25. I told him you were
        having writer's block — which is something
        he and I are familiar with.

Ernest Hemingway nods somberly in agreement.

                F.SCOTT FITZGERALD (CONT'D)
        Papa wanted to give you some advice.

>   ERNEST HEMINGWAY
> Don't call me Papa.
>
>   TYLER
> What's the advice?
>
>   ERNEST HEMINGWAY
> Don't think the answer is in the bottle.
>
>   TYLER
> I hate the taste of alcohol, wine and beer.
> I will never become an alcoholic like you
> two. It won't be a problem.

Fitzgerald and Hemingway look at each other, then
at Tyler, then they both burst out laughing.

>   ERNEST HEMINGWAY
> Have you introduced him to Gertrude Stein
> yet?

123

>   F.SCOTT FITZGERALD
> No. He's not ready for her, Papa.
>
>   ERNEST HEMINGWAY
> It'll be fun to watch. She'll chew him up
> alive. And don't call me Papa.
>
>   F.SCOTT FITZGERALD
> Meanwhile ... we've got to get a wiggle on.

Hemingway fist-bumps Tyler, then he and Fitzgerald
disappear. Tyler sits alone in the adjuncts office
and returns to the gift Andrew gave him.

INT. LORRAINE BANKS' OFFICE — DAY

Lorraine paces as she talks to someone we can't
see.

                    LORRAINE
Did Tyler's youth affect his performance?

                    FEMALE VOICE (O.S.)
His voice cracked a few times.

                    LORRAINE
Did he have a grasp of the material and did
you find his lecture compelling?

                    FEMALE VOICE (O.S.)
He drifted off on a few tangents, but when
he found his way back, he pretty much held
my attention.

                    LORRAINE
Did the rest of the class feel the same
way?

                    FEMALE VOICE (O.S.)
Overall.

                    LORRAINE
Is there anything about him that you feel
might be a problem?

                    FEMALE VOICE (O.S.)
One thing.

CLOSE ON the face of the girl who's been talking.

It's Hillary Pentella, the girl who dumped coffee
on Tyler. We see that she's serious and focused.

                    HILLARY
He's too nice. Nice might work in high
school, but here I can see it becoming
tedious. I need to be challenged, not niced
to death. Nice is for dogs.

124

> LORRAINE
> Thank you. I want your input so I can
> evaluate whether or not he's up to the job.
> I want you to come by and give me a report
> — especially these first three weeks.

Hillary nods to Lorraine, then leaves.

Lorraine considers the conversation for a moment,
then walks to the window and looks out. From her
expression she sees something.

LORRAINE'S POV

EXT. MANHATTAN COLLEGE — DAY

Tyler is leaving the building. As he approaches
the street he looks up and smiles broadly.

In the street is the tricked-out motorcycle we
saw earlier in Tyler's garage. Sitting on it is
his father, Angus.

> TYLER
> Dad!

> ANGUS
> Didn't seem right you takin' a bus home
> your first day. Hop on.

They hug, Angus hands Tyler a helmet, and both
get on the Harley.

BACK TO LORRAINE

She watches as Tyler and his father take off.

INT. TYLER'S BEDROOM — NIGHT

125

Tyler hangs the framed gift that Andrew gave him on the wall over his computer. When it's hung he looks at it and smiles.

CLOSE ON what the frame contains. We see a quotation on teaching.

> The mediocre teacher tells. The good teacher explains. The superior teacher demonstrates. The great teacher inspires.
> – William Arthur Ward

Tyler takes in the quote, then looks at the framed photograph of F. Scott Fitzgerald.

F. Scott Fitzgerald smiles and raises his martini glass in a toast.

FADE OUT

END OF SHOW

After reading the script, you've seen that all major characters have been introduced. You've gotten a sense of who the main character is, what he wants, what he's afraid of, his inner conflicts. You can see where the series can go.

The sample episodes in the proposal provide additional details as to the potential of the series.

writing exercise

Come up with five ideas for sitcoms. Bounce them off people you know who watch television. Get a consensus of which one they like best, then do an outline, and write the script and a proposal following my samples.

Something You Should Know That's Not Big Enough to Deserve Its Own Chapter

Webisodes and Vlogs

A webisode is a Web-based episodic video show. It's similar in structure to a television series, and new episodes are usually published on a periodic basis through a website or some other Internet-based medium.

Most shows have short runs (about five episodes) but some go longer. Because of their length, story is all-important. You have to get things rolling quickly. Another plus is that unlike prime-time television, you're not writing toward a commercial.

Popular webisodes include: *Smosh, Prom Queen, The Guild, Fred, Barats and Bareta, Dr. Horrible's Singalong Blog,* and *Clark and Michael.* Many prime-time shows have online webisodes too — *The Office, 30 Rock, Grey's Anatomy, Community,* and *Family Guy* to name a few.

Vlogs are an online diary or personal log of thoughts published on a Web page. Check out *LisaNova, Lonelygirl15, Katemodern.*

Because all you need to create a webisode or vlog is a camera, a script, and people to be in it, anyone can do it. It's kind of like the modern equivalent of a bunch of kids putting on a show in the barn.

Can you make money from them? Maybe. *Web Therapy,* starring Lisa Kudrow, has been picked up for a series on Showtime. Frankly, Lisa Kudrow is a big name with a great track record, but good things happen to unknowns too. *Barats and Bareta* got a pilot deal with NBC and a movie deal. And if we can creep into the world of Twitter, in 2009 Justin Halpern, a 28-year-old guy who moved back in with his parents, started tweeting the remarks of his 73-year-old father. He called it *Shit My Dad Says.* It caught on and was bought by CBS to be developed into a sitcom to star William Shatner.

127

But more than anything, creating webisodes or vlogs will give you experience. You'll learn how to squeeze a lot into a little time. You'll learn how to edit and revise and embellish. If you're going to appear in your webisode, you'll learn how to perform. Even if you're not an actor, by doing it you'll develop an understanding of how difficult it is to act, especially when you're saying original lines.

A Cautionary Tale
When You Get a Writing Job on a Sitcom, You're Going to Gain Weight

Besides the thrill of being hired as a writer on a sitcom, there are other perks, primarily free food. The writers' room tends to be adjacent to a kitchen that is fully stocked with food. Primarily junk food.

Even if you're making top dollar, you're still going to relish the free food. You also get free lunch. Most sitcom staffs never leave the building during lunch hour. You might go to your office to make a call or check your e-mail, but if the show is springing for lunch you'll hang around. The logic is that you'll eat for free, in the writers' room, and you'll pretty much work through lunch.

On the nights when the script is in trouble and you have to stay late, the show will also spring for dinner. And I'm not talking burgers and fries. I'm talking major food from fine dining restaurants.

On the first show I was on staff, I started at a pretty lean 192 pounds. Within 10 weeks I had ballooned up to 210. It took me four years to lose the weight.

So be forewarned.

THE MASTERS SPEAK

Wit is educated insolence.

— Aristotle

The duty of comedy is to correct men while amusing them.

— Moliere

I'd rather be a could-be if I cannot be an are; because a could-be is a maybe who is reaching for a star. I'd rather be a has-been than a might-have-been, by far; for a might-have-been has never been, but he was once an are.

— Milton Berle

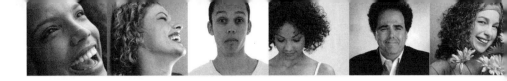

PART 4

STAND-UP

Don't tell jokes only the band laughs at.

— Milton Berle

The secret to humor is surprise.

— Aristotle

A poor joke must invent its own laughter.

— Proverb

Something You Should Know About Stand-Up That's Not Big Enough to Deserve Its Own Chapter

Immediacy

I'm in awe of stand-up comedians. They are the comedy equivalent of the long-distance runner. Alone with a microphone facing the unknown every time they walk on a stage. When a comic is just starting out, the stages are usually in grungy clubs.

The beauty of being a comic is the immediacy it provides for your creativity. You write a joke in the morning and you can perform it in front of an audience that night. It works or it doesn't. If it kills, you keep it and put it in your arsenal. If it bombs, you either put it down or keep working on it and you can try it again the next night. Still doesn't work? Play with it some more and try it again the next night. If it finally works, you keep it or you decide to let it go.

The only comedy-writing job where one gets some semblance of immediacy is if you're writing for a late night show when a joke or bit you've created that day might make it to the air that night.

As for sketches, they may never get on or you have to wait a few days (which is still good), but if you wrote a spec for a sitcom or a screenplay, you might wait years before it gets produced, if it all.

So relish the satisfaction of having the opportunity to have an instant reaction to your material. Other than when you're with your friends, you'll never find it anywhere else.

chapter 12

Going It Alone: The Unique World of Stand-Up Comics

I don't mean to sound bitter, cold or cruel,
but I am so that's how it comes out.

— Bill Hicks

There's a famous anecdote about a comedian performing in Las Vegas. He did two 60-minute shows a night: one at 9:30, the other at 11:30. One evening, after finishing his act, he's in his dressing room preparing to go home. There's a knock on the door. Standing there is a gorgeous, sexy 21-year-old girl holding a bottle of Champagne.

"You are the funniest, most brilliant comedian I've ever seen. You were turning me on for the entire show. I couldn't stop laughing. I had to meet you. I bought you this Champagne. I want you to come back to my hotel room and I want to make love to you all night long."

The comedian stared at her purposefully and unsmiling, then said, "Which show did you see?"

Such is the reality of the stand-up comic.

Why?

Because it's all about getting the laugh. It's not about getting sex or being complimented on your suit or cologne or new car. It's about the laugh.

Preferably an endless chain of laughs.

You may have seen a comedian on a talk show going on about how he or she is try-ing out new material in a small club in preparation for an upcoming HBO special. Never forget: That's what comedians do.

All comedians start out writing their own material. The great ones continue to write their own acts throughout their careers. Jerry Seinfeld does. So do Chris Rock and Dennis Miller. George Carlin wrote his material up until the very end. Others, upon attaining a certain level of success, hire people to write material for them, maybe not all, but some.

Nothing wrong with that. The objective is to have material for your act. Once you decide to enter the world of stand-up, it will be your prime objective. And it will be an all-consuming, ongoing process.

Stand-up comics need new material because an act can get stale fast, especially if you perform on television where a huge audience will see you. If you're doing five minutes on Letterman one night and Craig Ferguson in three weeks you can't use the same jokes.

So you have to find new material for your act. How do you do that?

Through observation, becoming a news junkie, listening to people, and waiting for the occasional burst of inspiration. Look to your friends, family, neighbors, girl-friends, boyfriends, the barista at your favorite Starbucks, newspapers, television, conversations overheard in restrooms, bars, and elevators.

In short: everywhere.

But the problem is that you can only use the material that is truthful to your comic persona.

What's that? Simply, it's the image or personality you convey to an audience.

Roseanne Barr burst onto the scene proclaiming herself as a domestic goddess. Her act was about the dark side of being a wife and mother. She was able to transfer that into one of the most successful sitcoms of all time.

Woody Allen was the socially inept, neurotic Jewish guy who can't get the girl.

Larry the Cable Guy is the redneck hillbilly.

Jack Benny was cheap.

Adam Sandler played guitar and sang comedy songs in his early stand-up routines.

Lisa Lampanelli takes no prisoners with her racial, cultural, and sexual barbs.

Louis C.K. does observational humor and is kind of an angry Jerry Seinfeld.

Richard Pryor used race and bigotry as the catalyst for his brilliant stand-up.

Patton Oswalt is the nerdy observer of a diverse range of subjects not even remotely connected.

The Amazing Jonathan combines comedy with magic, portraying a barely competent magician.

Bill Maher is political. So is Dennis Miller. In the '60s the political comedians were Mort Sahl and Lenny Bruce.

Jackie Mason has been drawing upon his Jewish heritage for more than 50 years.

Tim Allen started out with the maxim that all men's lives revolve around their tools. Like Roseanne, whose act dealt with her marriage and family, Tim's act was the catalyst for *Home Improvement*, the sitcom that made him a star.

In her stand-up days, Joan Rivers was ahead of her time with feminist, single girl in the big city humor.

Don Rickles made a career of insulting not only the members of his audiences, but celebrities as well. Before him there was Jack E. Leonard.

135

Rodney Dangerfield couldn't get any respect.

Before Dick Cavett became a talk show host he was a stand-up comic. He was born in Nebraska, but educated at Yale. His persona was the intellectual guy from the American farmland coping with the sophisticated big city.

Janeane Garofalo is the angry feminist liberal with the acerbic wit.

Richard Lewis' act was based on his many neuroses.

Sarah Silverman is outrageously foul-mouthed and pokes fun at religion, race, sex ... pretty much everything sacred, but in a witty, almost childlike manner.

Marc Maron is the angst-ridden, introspective observer of life.

quick exercise

Make a list of your favorite comedians. The best ones each have a style unique to them. A persona. And as you take your initial steps into the world of stand-up comedy, the first thing you must figure out is who you're going to be.

Maybe you already know.

The first thing any fledgling comic needs to deal with is his or her persona. Your act will come as a result of that. You may need to work at this until you find your comfort zone. For example, let's say you're a 23-year-old Italian guy and you have a bunch of eccentric but lovable relatives. You might decide that there's a wealth of material in them.

So you start with that and you get some laughs, but it doesn't quite work. So you decide to base your act on being a new dad. Or a recently divorced guy. Or a guy who has trouble with relationships. Or somebody overweight who talks about being fat and trying to lose weight.

Maybe you decide to crank things up and be blatantly raunchy with lots of sex and dick jokes. Or maybe you try observational humor or maybe you realize that having a more politically based act will work for you.

The point I'm making is that unless you know exactly the persona you're going to create, keep searching until either you find it or it finds you.

Maybe you're the fat guy who's going to make fun of his eating habits and inability to meet women. Or you're the overweight girl who'll do an about-face and build an act around how sexy and desirable you are. Or you're the nerdy Al Rokerish black guy who will play against all the stereotypes. Maybe you're the sexy blonde who'll feed off being the dumb blonde but will take it to a new level. Or you'll be the ex-professional. "I used to be a dentist/rabbi/proctologist" and you'll wrap your personality around your former career.

In the '80s, Yakov Smirnoff, a Russian immigrant, made a career out of being just that. His trademark line "What a country!" became a household expression.

When Drew Carey broke in he made fun of his geeky appearance.

Think of your favorite contemporary comedians. Imagine them when they were just starting out, trying to find their way, their look, their attitude, their point of view.

Point is, if you don't know what your persona should be, start looking inside yourself. Your persona will evolve. Sometimes your material will drive the persona; other times your persona drives the material. It's not something that can be taught. It has to be discovered. Maybe more than once. You try one way, and it doesn't feel right. You find another way. Almost there. You find another and another and another until you know who you are as a comedian.

When that happens, the quest to find material begins. If you're going to take it seriously, you'll constantly have your antennae up looking for inspiration.

Larry the Cable Guy has achieved enormous success. He didn't start out as the redneck with the thick Southern accent. He started out as himself: Dan Whitney. His real name. No accent. That persona didn't catch on. Somewhere along the line he found Larry or Larry found him.

Let's talk about Carrot Top for a moment. Although he's become something of a parody of himself, his act in Las Vegas is incredibly successful. He is what's known as a prop comedian. Instead of jokes, he's in a constant struggle to come up with new ideas for inane props. Then he has to build them and try them out on stage and see if they get laughs. If they do, they stay in his act. If they don't, they're gone.

Just as Carrot Top uses his brain to find ideas for his props, you must use your brain to find ideas for jokes.

Carry a notebook with you at all times to write down even the most fleeting of thoughts, ideas, and notions. If you don't write them down, you'll forget them.

Trust me. You *will* forget them.

You may end up tossing three-quarters of them, but the ones you keep will be the building blocks of your act.

137

Your Act

Depending on what stage in your career you are, your "act" can be as short as three minutes or up to an hour. Once you attain superstar status, your act can extend from 90 minutes to two hours.

When you're new to the game, finding enough material to fill three minutes of stage time is like climbing Mount Everest barefoot. How long is three minutes? Look at your wristwatch and count them off. Just sit in silence wherever you are right now and stare at your watch as 180 seconds go by. Okay. Now imagine that you're in a comedy club filled with people who are there to be entertained. Now imagine having enough amusing things to say to keep them laughing for three minutes. Or 10 minutes. Or 20. Or 60. Or longer.

Once you start developing material that works, your act takes shape. Let's say you have five to seven minutes on a particular topic. This is called a "chunk." Unless your act will consist of a string of jokes, one-liners, and quick observations, you will need to develop chunks. If you're allotted 15 minutes of stage time, you might use three chunks.

Assignment

Study the acts of your favorite comics. Time them. See how many chunks they have. See who doesn't use any. See how they fit them into their act.

What If Your Material Isn't Working?

What do you do if your material isn't funny? Instead of laughs you get unforgiving stares or a random chortle from one person in the corner. Getting no or very few laughs is called "dying."

Ironically, when you get the big belly laughs and every second of your material is greeted not only with laughter, but with applause, it means that you "killed" or that you "knocked 'em dead" or that you "slayed 'em."

Depending upon the audience, a comedian who *kills* one night can *die* the next despite using the same material. Working comics often refer to their act as their "A and B Material." "A Material" refers to his best jokes that will demonstrate his wit, hipness, and intelligence. "B Material" is more-generic jokes. Maybe not as current or cool, but can be "gotten" by a less hip, sophisticated, or informed crowd.

Why do some jokes work and others don't?

Below is a list of potential joke-killers. You'll see that it's similar to what makes a sketch not work.

The Setup Is Unclear
The audience isn't sure what the premise of the joke is.

The Setup Is Ambiguous
You have more than one premise. You risk confusing the audience.

You Go Off on a Tangent
Your setup is clear, but as you get into the joke, you go off on a tangent or lose the primary dramatic thrust.

Too Many Beats
You're getting too complicated and an audience can't follow where you're heading. Let the audience come with you.

Your Timing Is Off
The biggest laugh-killer. Not knowing when to pause, how long to hold back, and not stepping on your own lines. This will come with lots of practice and stage time.

That Old Devil Political Correctness

Be aware of the politically correct factor. Don't cross a line and lose a laugh or, worse, say something that alienates your audience. Some audiences will be with you if you use foul language, gross-out humor, and sex jokes. Others will be turned off or pissed off. Practice will help you gauge your audiences.

Bad Grammar

Make sure you pronounce words correctly. Don't have a laugh go south because of poor sentence structure or phrasing.

The Cool Factor

Don't try to be too cool, smug, or esoteric. And don't sound like you're begging for a laugh.

Should You Work Blue?

Using foul language in a comedian's act is referred to as "working blue." Historically, many comics had material they performed on television that was clean, but when they appeared in Vegas or nightclubs they got raunchier. Others established reputations as working clean. Still others had acts that were blatantly off-color (Richard Prior, Andrew Dice Clay, Sam Kinison).

It's still pretty much that way, but there are far more comics, men and women, whose acts are laced with profanity and foul language.

This is your choice. It works for some, but not for others.

What do you do when you've figured out your comic persona and managed to write a few minutes of material?

Time to go to a comedy club, right? Wrong. Not yet. First, audiotape or videotape yourself. It's important to hear what you sound like and see what you look like. You need to appear confident, even if you're scared out of your mind (and you will be the first few times).

Don't tell the audience that it's your first time. They don't need to know that.

And don't be hard on yourself if you don't get many (or any) laughs. It'll probably be your first time speaking in front of an audience. Studies show that the fear of public speaking is considered to be the No. 1 fear of people in the United States. So for you to get up on a stage and stand before a group of strangers just might be a little traumatizing.

Remember this: You're not there to speak. You're there to say funny things.

Speaking of strangers, bring along someone who cares about you. Don't bring a group of friends or coworkers yet. Just one person. Someone to ride home with you and be supportive.

It's also a good idea to record your sets. Not only to help you remember the material that worked (or didn't), but so you can hear how you sound. Are you talking too loud, fast, slowly, or softly? Is your pacing off? Doing this will help you realize which areas need the most work. Place a tape recorder backstage or close enough for you to hear yourself. If you can videotape yourself it's even better.

And for your first few times on stage, try to find a "friendly" microphone, i.e., a club or venue that's not too large. The audiences for most open mic nights are mainly other fledgling comedians, not necessarily the most welcoming of audiences.

Okay. It's time to hit a comedy club. Most have open mic nights. Sign up and go on stage. You probably won't be "killing" your audience. Most likely you'll be "dying."

You'll "die" a lot more often than you'll "kill" when you first start out.

140

You'll learn more by not getting laughs than by getting them. What sounded so funny at your computer or as you paced around your living room or as you watched the video you made will sound different after you've said it to a crowd. Comics never bother to analyze *why* something gets a laugh. The hard part is trying to figure out why something *doesn't* get a laugh.

Is it the timing? Is it over your audience's collective head? Is it a joke that an audience has heard before from someone else? Are the jokes in the wrong order? Is it too confusing? Are you talking too loud? Too soft? Do you come off as unprepared? Are you too confident? Do you start off strong and then get increasingly less funny? Or is your material weak and boring until the last 30 seconds, but by that point you've lost your audience so it's an example of too little too late?

These are the questions stand-up comics ask themselves on a daily basis. After a show they wonder why certain jokes didn't get laughs. The next day when they're working on new material they wonder which of the latest output will get laughs and which won't.

That's the life of a comic.

But after you've "killed" for the first time you'll get a taste for it. It's a worthwhile, rewarding career that can lead to success in other venues.

You also get to sleep late every day.

Something You Should Know Once You Start Getting Gigs

Performing

In every show there's an Emcee, a Middle, and a Headliner. The Emcee warms up the crowd and sets the tone. The Middle, which is considered the best spot, usually just does his or her material. The Headliner is the real pro and brings it all home.

Think of the Emcee as the sacrificial lamb. No one knows how the crowd will be until the first comic gets up there. There's always an energy you can feel, but you can't tell for sure how receptive an audience will be until you start talking.

On a venue with more comics, the Emcee comes out before each performer and does a few minutes. Consider this your journeyman work. But your immediate goal is to move up to the Middle. If the Emcee has done his job and warmed up the crowd, as the Middle you'll face an audience that's primed to laugh. If the Emcee has crashed and burned, you're on your own.

Part of the Middle's job is to further warm up the audience for the Headliner. You do that and you're done for the night.

Becoming the Headliner is the next step. You get the most stage time and the most money.

Lastly, whether you're the Emcee or the Middle, you'll be allotted a certain amount of time.

Don't go over it.

Your job is to warm up and prepare the audience for the Headliner. An audience can only take so much comedy. They can only sit so long before they start to sag.

If you're told to do 15 minutes, don't do 40, because you'll burn out the crowd for the Headliner.

How to Write a Joke

There are different kinds of jokes.

There's the old school Henny Youngman one-liner: "Take my wife. *Please!*" And we get a different kind of one-liner from one of my favorite comics, Steven Wright: "I almost had a psychic girlfriend but she left me before we met."

There's the current-event joke that a late night host might say. For example, in the spring of 2010 Kitty Kelley published her gossipy biography of Oprah Winfrey. Here's one way to make a joke about that.

"So Kitty Kelley's tell-all biography of Oprah Winfrey was published today. I guess that's one book that won't be making Oprah's Book Club."

Then there's the classic Rule of 3 joke: "I love going to New Orleans. They have the best food and music in the world. All I want to do is eat. Last time I was there I was so hungry I ate three bowls of gumbo, six catfish po-boys, and that mole over Aaron Neville's eye."

Let's go back to the observational humor. Most jokes are grounded in that. Jerry Seinfeld is the master. Here's one of his: "I was the best man at the wedding. If I'm the best man, why is she marrying him?"

How about Marc Maron on marriage: "If you don't have a woman in your life keeping you down, you have no perspective."

How many stand-up acts revolve around relationships? Newly married, long married, single, newly divorced, considering marriage, afraid of marriage, dating problems, sex, lack of sex, meeting crazy women, meeting crazy guys, second marriages, dating younger women, dating older guys, having a baby, being a new parent and how it changes a relationship.

Next come dysfunctional families, relatives, and in-laws, then bad habits, addictions, and neuroses. For some it's politics and social causes.

The best comics draw on their own lives. Comedy has to come from a place of realism. Audiences laugh at things they can relate to. Every guy has had the crazy girlfriend. Every woman has had the nightmare date from hell. Most people keep their thoughts to themselves, but when a comic taps into something that resonates — something that a person in the audience has *thought* about but never expressed — he's going to get a laugh or smile or, at the very least, that appreciative nod of recognition.

How many times have you nodded your head in agreement when you heard a comic make an observation that hit home with you (and the rest of the audience)?

I can't "teach" you how to write a good joke any more than I can "teach" you how to make good chili. I can give you the formula or recipe, but then it's up to you to put it all together and make it work.

What's the formula?

Go into your own life. Not only the present, but the past. Look especially at the paradox and irony of life. The unfairness and incongruity. The silly little things that turn into big things. The tangents of life. I heard radio personality Jonathan Schwartz say that life is a bitter mystery. That resonated with me. The older we get, the less life makes sense. I thought I had all the answers when I was 25. Unfortunately, most of the time I was asked the wrong question.

When constructing a joke, try to keep the words to a minimum. One or two sentences to give the audience the information they need to *follow* and *get* the joke.

Create the setup at the get-go and pay off the joke in another sentence or a few sentences, depending on whether you're telling something anecdotally. Taking too long to get to the payoff could hurt you because the audience will get tired of waiting.

143

Think setup and payoff, setup and payoff, setup and payoff. Or setup, payoff, topper. The "topper" is the second joke that feeds off the previous punchline or payoff. The *second* topper is the next joke that feeds off the first topper, so it needs no new setup line. You might even have a third or fourth topper.

Start with a premise:

(**Setup**) "The cashier at the supermarket I go to judges me when I buy junk food. If I have a box of Twinkees, bag of Funyons and a pint of Chunky Monkey ice cream, she'll give me a look that says 'That shit's not gonna solve your problems, loser.'"(**Payoff**)

(**Setup**) "The first few times she gave me that look I pointed at the junk food and casually said, 'It's for my kids.' She didn't exactly roll her eyes, but she was clearly thinking of rolling her eyes. Once she had the audacity to say, 'Is your kid gonna drink that 12-pack of Corona?' (**Topper**) (**Setup**) It's gotten to the point where I feel she sees right through me. Kind of like my mother. Kind of like my ex-wife. Kind of like the woman who just dumped me and is the reason I'm consuming 7,000 empty calories a day. (**Topper**) (**Setup**) Sometimes, to avoid her, I'll go to the cashier next to her with a stash of food that only a 300-pound teenager in a trailer camp would love. **(Topper)** **(Setup)** I glanced in her direction. We made eye contact. She looked at my frozen onion rings, family-size bag of Doritos, and king-size container of Cheese Whiz and shook her head back and forth as if I were going to barbecue a small dog." **(Topper)**

One of the hardest things to learn is timing. New comics need to know how to wait for the laugh and understand the value of the pause. A truly refined act is perfected down to the second. Often when a comic gets a booking on a late night show she's given four minutes. She then has to take one of her five-, six- or seven-minute chunks and edit it down. Not easy to do.

Specifics are always better than generalities. In the above I mentioned a "pint of Chunky Monkey" ice cream. I could have just said "ice cream" or "chocolate ice cream," but using a real, funny-sounding name sweetens the joke.

Don't let your audience get ahead of you. Be original and creative enough that the audience doesn't know the punchline halfway through.

Something You Should Know

Podcast: The Evolution of Radio

Ten years ago I would've said that another great venue for comedy writing is to write material for radio personalities. But then came satellite radio in the form of XM and Sirius.

I listened to Howard Stern for 20 years, then he moved to Sirius and to hear him his fans had to pay. Some went along for the ride; some didn't.

Time passed. XM and Sirius merged. More and more radio personalities jumped from terrestrial radio and more major markets cut back on their on-air talent. For our purposes here, I'm referring to the many "funny" morning or afternoon drive-time personalities or shock jocks in most major markets.

145

These people still exist around the country, but there are far fewer now. How does that affect you as a comedy writer? If you live in a major market with a local comedy radio personality, you have the opportunity to submit comedy material to him or her. Most write their own stuff or have a couple of sidekicks who help come up with bits, jokes, and whatnot. But these guys still need material. So if you had ideas or fully written-out bits, you could submit them. Maybe you'd sell one or two. And then more. And if you were really good you might get a steady gig out of it. I did this with Don Imus. Material I wrote got on the air.

But as I write this in 2010, there's talk that satellite radio is on the way out. I'm beginning to think that the future of "radio" is in the form of the podcast.

What's a podcast? A series of digital media files, either audio or video, that are released episodically and downloaded through Web syndication. I go to iTunes for mine.

In the last year some radio personalities who lost their jobs have started doing podcasts. My favorite is Adam Carolla, formerly of *The Man Show*, *Crank Yankers*, and *Loveline*, author and star of *The Hammer*, and host of a morning radio program in Los Angeles. In 2009 his show was cancelled.

Shortly thereafter he started a daily podcast at his personal website. In the initial 24 hours, the first Adam Carolla podcast was downloaded over 250,000 times and, as of the third podcast, it was the No. 1 podcast on iTunes in both the U.S. and Canada.

During its debut week, *The Adam Carolla Podcast* recorded over a million downloads. In the second week it recorded over 2 million. I was listening to him from the first day.

As he learned about the nature of podcasts, so did I.

So did other comedians. Within the next eight to 10 months, more podcasters started to appear. *WTF* with Marc Maron is terrific. So are Greg Fitzsimmons, David Feldman, and Jimmy Pardo (*Never Not Funny*). Filmmaker Kevin Smith has one that's fun called *Smodcast* that's worth checking out. As the months pass, you'll find more and more funny people getting into this burgeoning field.

146

How does this affect you?

Maybe you should start a podcast. You won't have access to the caliber of guests that Adam Carolla and the other established comedians can get, but you'll have a venue to test material.

That's what it's all about in the beginning for comedy writers. Getting experience, whether it's writing or performing.

Podcasts are essentially the host talking and pontificating. What they say tends to be funny. It's all ad-libbed. Do you think you can talk spontaneously for an hour? Maybe you should try it. I should caution you that starting a podcast isn't cheap. Carolla has stated that the bandwidth necessary to get the job done costs over $9,000 a month.

What's bandwidth? It's too complicated to explain. I suggest Googling *wisegeek. com* for a clear explanation.

Go to iTunes and check out the variety of podcasts available. Listen and study and then decide if this is something that could be right for you.

THE MASTERS SPEAK

The Four Levels of Comedy: Make your friends laugh, Make strangers laugh, Get paid to make strangers laugh, and Make people talk like you because it's so much fun.

— Jerry Seinfeld

True humor springs not more from the head than from the heart. It is not contempt; its essence is love. It issues not in laughter, but in still smiles, which lie far deeper.

— Thomas Carlyle

Someone who makes you laugh is a comedian. Someone who makes you think and then laugh is a humorist.

— George Burns

PART 5

Screenwriting

Your joy is sorrow unmasked. And the
self-same well from which your laughter rises
was often-times filled with your tears.

— Rene Descartes

chapter 13

Writing Short Comedy Screenplays (For *Funny or Die* and Other Comedy Websites)

No mind is thoroughly well organized that is deficient in a sense of humor.

— Samuel Taylor Coleridge

Before you attempt to write a full-length comedy, start with a one- or two-minute script. There are some great venues to show your work.

At the beginning of 2005 nobody had heard of YouTube. By the end of 2006 the company was bought by Google for $1.65 billion. In its short existence it has become the new showcase for wannabe comedy writers, filmmakers, and performers.

Will Ferrell took comedy on the Internet to the next level when he created *Funny or Die*. If you're not familiar with *Funny or Die*, check it out. It's a venue for people who've made short comedies to get them seen.

Funny or Die and other sites like it give you a chance to get your work up for viewing. When you're embarking on a career as a sketch writer, unless you're hooked up with an improvisational group or comedy troupe that will mount your sketches, you won't have the opportunity to see your work performed.

With the availability of inexpensive cameras, anybody can make a movie and have a place to get it seen. If a short film is any good, it could be recommended and many, many people would get to see it. And the creators of the best of the best could actually launch their careers.

Remember this: A short comedy is in reality a sketch that's filmed. Most sketches on TV have one set. When you're *filming* a sketch, you have the option of opening it up and taking your camera outside, to other locations or anywhere. Or not. You can shoot it in your grandmother's kitchen.

But basically you're writing a sketch, so the same rules of sketch writing apply. *Like a sketch,* the best short films have a story with a beginning, middle, and ending.

You'll be writing your short script in the screenplay format. If you're not familiar with this, it's pretty basic. I suggest ordering Final Draft Screenwriting Software to make your life easier, or Google "screenplay format" for more information. Until then, here are the basics.

Tell us where the scene takes place (the slug line). Tell us who's in the scene with very brief character descriptions. (Why? When I read a screenplay I like to know who I'm looking at.) Tell us what the character or characters are doing (the action, sometimes called stage directions or screen directions). Use all capital letters for the names of characters when you introduce them. For the rest of the script, don't use all capitals for names. Always have at least one line describing what's going on in the scene.

INT. KITCHEN — DAY

KRISTA, 16, cute, studious, insecure about her looks, sits across from ANGIE, 19, her hot, ditzy, overly made-up sister. Angie's doing her nails; Krista's peeling potatoes.

After this basic description it's all about the dialogue.

Center the character name (3" in Word). And set the dialogue margin at 1.5". I suggest investing in a screenwriting program. I recommend Final Draft. It does everything for you except write the script.

When one scene ends, move on to the next scene.

EXT. KRISTA AND ANGIE'S BACKYARD — DAY

Angie is sunning herself. Krista is raking leaves.

More dialogue.

When this scene ends, go to the next scene.

How many scenes should there be? As many as the story you want to tell requires. But remember: You're writing a *short* screenplay, maybe five to seven pages, so you can't have 148 scenes. Maybe you'll need six scenes or 10 or two or only one. If your ultimate goal is to make a two- or three-minute movie, we're not talking all that many scenes.

Obviously, in your script the characters will be talking about *something*, i.e., whatever the story is. And as discussed in the sketch chapter, get the story started quickly.

In the above scenario, Krista and Angie are in their kitchen, but they can't just be talking about the weather. Something has to get the story started. In a full-length screenplay (discussed in detail in the next chapter), you can take three or four pages before getting the story started. In the short screenplays you'll be writing you don't have that luxury. You have to get the premise introduced immediately.

So we FADE IN on Krista and Angie in their kitchen. Krista's peeling potatoes; Angie's doing her nails.

                    ANGIE
     I don't get how you can be a freakin' vegetarian.

                    KRISTA
     Meat and fish are living things. I can't in
     all good conscience eat something that has
     parents.

                    ANGIE
     A tuna fish doesn't have parents.

                    KRISTA
     How do you think a tuna fish got created?

                    ANGIE
     They just come in the can.

Krista rolls her eyes.

This brief exchange is the setup for a short film about two sisters who are polar opposites.

And that's the format.

Don't waste space using CUT TO after every scene. And don't put a lot of description in your stage directions.

When you write a short comedy, all you need is a camera, some friends, and not too much money, and you're ready to go. You're like a stand-up comic who writes a joke in the morning and gets to see how it works that night. Once you've edited it you can upload it to any number of websites. And if it's really good, i.e., really funny, it'll get word of mouth, and if you're really lucky it'll go viral and who knows what kind of attention you will get.

assignment

Check out the following comedy websites and see the type of short screenplays other people have done. The best ones all have something in common: a story.

Maybe the acting isn't great and the sound could be better and it's underlit or overlit, but that can be forgiven if there's a story that hooks you.

Funnyordie.com

Atom.com

Comedytime.tv

Break.com

Funnycomedyvideos.com

Collegehumor.com

Nationallampoon.com

Icomedytv.com

chapter 14

Writing the Full-Length
Comedy Screenplay:
What's the
Right Genre for You?

*Imagination was given to man to
compensate him for what he is not; a sense
of humor to console him for what he is.*

— Francis Bacon

155

As I've made it clear, just because you can say funny things doesn't mean you can *write* funny things. Writing a spec script for a half-hour sitcom means writing roughly 30 to 35 pages of funny dialogue.

It's hard. You'll see.

Writing a spec sitcom pilot is even harder because you don't have characters someone else has created. You have to create the characters, the premise, et al., and on top of that it has to be filled with funny dialogue.

Writing a full-length screenplay is like writing three original pilots. I encourage my screenwriting students to shoot for 110 pages.

Before you do anything you'll need to learn the structure of a screenplay. Below is a crash course presented in the language of texting and Twitter:

Twitter for Screenwriters

- OMG. Get your story started fast.

- Have the Instigating Event (or Inciting Incident if you prefer) happen ASAP — within Pages 1-4.

- The Instigating Event is the thing that makes the rest of the movie happen.

- Make sure The Major Dramatic Question is clear by the end of Act 1.

- Justify every line of dialogue and every scene. If there's no dramatic purpose for a line or scene, cut it.

- Make sure you know *what* your main character wants, why he wants it now, *what* does he have to do to get it, and what will happen if he *doesn't* get it.

- Major Dramatic Question: Will boy get girl? Will the cop find the killer? Will ET get home? Will they kill the monster?

- Give your main character an Ear: someone to talk to and listen to. His BFF, brother, roommate, coworker, et al.

- Have plenty of complications in Act 2. Don't make things too easy for your protagonist. Whatever he wants must be hard to get.

- BTW. Get your subplot rolling early in Act 2.

- Remember: Almost every film ever made has a romantic subplot. Yours should too. Don't believe me? Watch a bunch of movies. You'll find one in 99%.

- Always have a middle of Act 2 event that cranks up the action. Approximately Page 55.

- Have a big moment at the end of Act 2 that propels the story into Act 3. Think of it as introducing new information, something unexpected.

- Have another event in the middle of Act 3 that further cranks up the action.

- Aim for a satisfying ending. Doesn't have to be happy, but it should be satisfying.

- After your first draft, get feedback from AFPOE (3 is best). Do a rewrite, then get feedback from your most trusted friend. Do a polish.

- After the polish, don't look at it for at least a few weeks. Longer if possible. The distance will give you clarity. Then do a final pass.

- You are done.

- Focus on trying to find an agent, manager, or producer to read your script.

- Start your next screenplay and repeat the process.

a quick lesson

The Punctuation Theory of Screenwriting

The end of Act 1 ends with a question mark. (?)

The end of Act 2 ends with an exclamation point. (!)

The end of Act 3 ends with a period. (.)

By the end of Act 1 (ideally Pages 30-34) the Major Dramatic Question *must* be clear. The person reading the script must know what the story is.

Think of the end of Act 2 exclamation point as new information, a surprise, something you didn't expect. It should be powerful enough to propel the reader into Act 3. You've seen many completed films that have a weak end of Act 2 moment. The best ones come as a complete surprise.

No matter what the genre, Act 3 should be the most exciting. The Major Dramatic Question must be answered. Once it's answered the story has ended and it's time to go home. In some scripts, though, the Major Dramatic Question is answered at the end of Act 2. This is too early to end, so the Major Dramatic Question changes as you get into Act 3.

Think of Acts 1 and 2 as the ride up in a roller coaster. Think of Act 3 as the ride down.

The Wave Movement

Stand on an ocean beach and look at the waves. They all start way out, but most peter out. However, some get started and keep moving, growing in size and speed as they come *crashing* into shore.

That's what your screenplay should be like. It must build and build and build until ...

157

a quick lesson

Watch *The Crying Game* (1992, written and directed by Neil Jordan). In my opinion it has the greatest end of Act 2 moment in the history of film.

a longer exercise. really longer

From this moment on for the rest of your life, every time you watch a movie (be it in a theater or at home), pay close attention to the end of Act 1, but *especially* the end of Act 2 event. You'll be surprised at how many films don't deliver the goods. There might be a clear-cut end of Act 2 moment, but it's so predictable you probably saw it coming 20 minutes into the movie.

However, the films that deliver the goods, that make you smile in surprise, will add another level of enjoyment to your viewing experience.

Let's Focus on Writing Comedies

So you're funny in real life with your friends, family, and coworkers. They're the ones you've been unofficially playing to and they've probably been an easy audience.

As the author of a screenplay that's a comedy, your audience will be much tougher and unforgiving: agents, producers, development people, creative executives, and managers.

You have to keep that agent laughing from the first page — *especially* the first page — because if she's enjoying herself by the time she gets to the bottom, she'll definitely turn to Page 2. And if you keep the laughs coming for the next 10 pages and the rest of the first act, you can feel pretty confident she'll finish the entire script — provided you have a compelling story.

Understand this: A strong story without a lot of laughs is preferable to a weak story with five jokes per page.

Many comedies falter because of a flimsy or dimwitted plot. Ultimately, no matter how many laughs a script has, if the story isn't absorbing enough for somebody to sink her teeth into, it won't get read to the final Fade Out. As we're laughing at things your characters are saying and doing, we must *care* about them and root for them to get whatever it is they want (no matter how goofy). If that want isn't there, we aren't going along for that ride no matter how amusing it might be.

There's an old maxim in baseball: "I'd rather be lucky than talented." When it comes to a comedy screenplay, I'd rather have a solid story than plenty of laughs. Laughs can be put in. Maybe not by you, but if it's a great story, your chance of getting an agent or a deal has just gotten closer to the goal line.

Another old sports saying is: "You can't teach speed."

If you've written a 103-page script with plenty of laughs but you have a weak, mediocre, or nonsensical story, well, just as "you can't teach speed," I'll expand on that and say, "You can't punch up a weak plot" without starting from scratch. In the industry, that's called a Page One Rewrite and this happens all the time to screenplays that have been bought and are slated for production. That's why there will be the occasional movie poster listing four or more screenwriters (and odds are there were a few more who didn't get screen credit).

Let's say you're seriously considering writing screenplays (comedies or any genre, but let's focus on comedies). You have a good understanding of not only the three-act structure, but five-act and seven-act structures, as well. You know that characters should be three-dimensional, have internal and external conflicts, and be properly motivated.

159

You've immersed yourself in *Writers Journey*, by Christopher Vogler, so you know the 12 Stages of the Hero's Journey inside and out. You've read all the screenwriting books (especially mine, *The Screenwriter Within*), gone to seminars, studied, analyzed, and deconstructed films, read the key biographies and autobiographies of screen-writers, and subscribed to the best screenwriting magazines.

But despite that, you're incapable of writing funny dialogue.

Conversely, what are you supposed to do if you have no trouble coming up with dialogue, but you can't find a good story? Unfortunately, all the ideas you come up with are way too serious and downbeat (like that bio-pic on Damien the Leper you've been mulling over the last three years).

If you fall into either of these categories, you might need a collaborator.

Two Heads Can Be Better Than One

For some, it's the perfect convergence of talent.

Check the credits on sitcoms. You'll find at least one and often two or three writing teams on every show. Same with screenplays. It's fair to assume that most of these teams got together because they each brought their strength to the table.

Finding your writing soul mate isn't easy. It's like finding someone to marry. You have to look around, see how you get on, and hope that it works. If it does work, you'll both be in a much better place than going it alone.

This is not to say that some writing teams consist of people who are adept at story and funny dialogue and the reason they're collaborating is because they need someone to bounce ideas off or for the discipline or for whatever reason.

But if you're lacking in one area, find a partner lacking in your strength and you're on your way.

If you don't want to collaborate and if your heart is set on writing comedies, all I can say is that you should keep staring at the scene that needs punching up until a funny line pops into your head. Then do it again and again and again. Just don't try to analyze what's funny or figure out where it comes from.

A typical scene in a screenplay is as long as a sketch. Look over the chapter on sketch writing and try some of those exercises. If you force yourself to learn to write funny and stick with it and practice, it just might help you turn a corner.

Finding Your Genre

Whether you're going to work alone or collaborate with someone, finding your genre is the next step.

When we go to a Farrelly brothers movie we expect a certain kind of product. Gross-out humor in largely unrealistic, high-concept plots with a handful of genuinely inspired lines and moments. Woody Allen films, especially his early and mid-career efforts, offered a witty, neurotic take on the human condition, especially romance. His fans knew that they were going to see a unique, intellectual kind of creativity and wit. If Judd Apatow's name is on a film, be it as writer, producer, or director, we know it'll be something high concept with an abundance of sex jokes, but with an undertone of sweetness.

The thing is, depending upon the kind of comedy you're writing, you may not need to be as funny as these guys. Romantic comedies need laughs, but not necessarily six per page. Take two Reese Witherspoon films. *Sweet Home Alabama* wasn't a laugh a minute. Neither was *Legally Blonde*, although it was funnier and had a higher concept. But both had compelling stories.

Guy comedies (or buddy comedies) need more laughs than romantic comedies.

Think *The Hangover*; *I Love You, Man*; *Wedding Crashers*; *The Pineapple Express*; or *Role Models*.

Comedy screenplays are allowed to have some laying-pipe sections, but not many. And there should be none in the first 15 pages. You have to keep the laughs coming.

So if you want to write a big, broad comedy (*The Hangover*; *Tropic Thunder*; *Dodgeball*; *Liar, Liar*), your script better be funny as hell from first page to last.

If you want to write a romantic comedy or something serio-comic (serious topic with laughs) or a comedy/drama (lighthearted story with a serious or sentimental turn), you don't necessarily have to have three to six laughs per page. Once again, here is where having a solid story will supersede lots of laughs.

Ultimately, the biggest obstacle to writing a full-length comedy is the idea. Lots of comedies are written (and made) that have weak, soft, or stupid ideas. Coming up with that unique premise will be a huge plus. And if you can tell the story and make it funny and entertaining, that'll be another thing in your favor.

But trust me: Finding that great/cool/genius idea isn't easy. And even if you manage to come up with one, unless it's properly executed, you're screwed. I can't tell you how many great ideas I've heard from students over the years. But the execution was weak.

161

Likewise, I've also heard many, many ideas that were tepid and pretty uninspired, but the execution was amazing.

So what's the lesson? Great idea with poor execution? Nada. Weak idea with great execution? You have a shot.

WARNING!!!

Here comes another cooking analogy.

Learning to write comedies is pretty much like learning to cook. If you take cooking classes, read a bunch of cookbooks, watch The Food Network, and spend enough time in the kitchen trying out recipes, you'll be able to prepare a meal that you won't be ashamed of. You may even get really good at it.

Read books on comedy writing (*Writing the Romantic Comedy* is very good, as is *What Are You Laughing At: How to Write Funny Screenplays, Stories, and More*). What's also very helpful is to watch and *study* comedies (you'll learn more from the bad ones than the good). And don't limit yourself to contemporary films.

Go back. Watch films from the last 80 years. Educate yourself to what people were watching when your parents, grandparents, or great-grandparents were going to the movies.

Some are timeless; others are of their time. The deeper your knowledge of film history (in your case, comedy), the better writer you'll be.

Some Pointers on Outlining Your Screenplay

I always ask students to write a short outline or three-act breakdown of their story *before* they start writing the script. The purpose of this is to force you to think your story through. You might change things once you start writing the script, but it's good to have a blueprint or map of where the story is going.

What follows are examples, each of different lengths, of four ideas for a screenplay, written by me.

SMOTHERED WITH ONIONS

A 112-pound nutritionist falls for a guy who likes fat women. Against her better judgment, she decides to put on weight. Because she's into health, she has difficulty gaining weight, so she hires an overweight guy (one of her clients) to help her eat badly. After putting on 48 pounds she realizes she's gained more than she bargained for.

Short and to the point. You get the idea of what it's about.

Here's another, a bit longer:

THE BRAINIAC

A high school teacher's worst-ever student (now 25) comes back into his life and wants him to teach him all the stuff he never learned in school. He wants this in order to impress a highly intelligent woman he's met who has a Ph.D. and is a college professor. He feels he'll lose her because he's not smart enough.

Initially the teacher says no. He hated the guy when he was his student. But the twist is that the student is now hugely successful and offers to pay him. Because the teacher is deeply in debt due to his spendaholic habits, he agrees to help the guy. The further twist is that the teacher, upon meeting the woman, realizes that he's more right for her than the student, so he decides to sabotage the learning process.

Here's one that's even more thought-out:

DASHING THROUGH THE SNOW

PREMISE

A guy registers with an online dating service that promises to find his perfect match. They set him up with a beautiful, intelligent woman and he falls for her instantly. She falls for him too. They are indeed each other's perfect match. Only problem is that she claims to be the daughter of Santa Claus and she has a secret reason for wanting a husband.

OUTLINE

CHRISTIE KRINGLE registers with the Perfect Match online dating service. She's interested in a man who meets the following criteria:

- A guy who's overweight (or a guy who wouldn't mind putting on weight).
- A guy who likes cold weather.
- A guy who can grow a full beard.
- A guy with a hearty laugh.
- A guy with leadership skills.
- A guy with a pilot's license.
- A guy with strong feelings about Christmas.

163

RANDY ELWAY registers with Perfect Match because he's tired of going through another holiday season (his favorite time of year) without a date for the many Christmas parties he's invited to.

His requests are simple: a woman who enjoys the holiday season, likes to sit around warm fireplaces or go caroling and for winter sleigh rides in the country.

Christie is told that her perfect match is Randy. Randy is told that his perfect match is Christie.

They meet. She's gorgeous. He falls for her instantly. She falls for him too, initially because he meets all the criteria she requires. They go on a date and she tells him that she's the last living descendant of Santa Claus. He thinks she's nuts.

Then she tells him that in the bylaws of the North Pole, only a man can be Santa Claus, which is why she can't take over. However, there's a loophole that says the husband of Santa's daughter can also become Santa Claus. She explains that her father, the current Santa Claus, must take mandatory retirement and that unless she marries a man who can take over, there will be no Christmas.

Christie tells Randy that if he marries her he must become Santa Claus.

Now he really thinks she's crazy. He tells her he can't go out with her anymore. He hires a private detective to do a genealogy search on Christie.

Meanwhile, as he looks at his life, he starts to wonder if becoming Santa Claus wouldn't be so bad, if it meant being with Christie.

The major complication is that Christie has found another possible candidate in the form of a professional department store Santa named CECIL DELLAFORCIA. Not only does he look and sound exactly like Santa, he'd be perfect for the job.

Only problem is, he's not a very nice guy. He's like an actor who plays a lovable guy on a sitcom, but in real life is obnoxious. But because Christie has the responsibility of finding the next Santa, she feels she must marry him.

When Randy hears about this he realizes he can't let her marry this nasty guy, so he must dash through the snow to the North Pole to marry Christie before she can marry Cecil.

Near the end, the private detective shows up with some powerful information that saves the day.

And here is what I feel is the strongest way to present your story. A three-act breakdown:

GRACE BEFORE MEALS

PREMISE

A woman who is helpless in the kitchen and has no interest in cooking falls head over heels for a food writer who values a woman's ability to cook over everything else. She pretends she knows how to cook to win his heart only to have this backfire on her when he asks her to cook Thanksgiving dinner for his family.

THREE-ACT BREAKDOWN

Act 1

GRACE, 25, likes to joke that she comes from a long line of women who can't cook, burn food, and start kitchen fires. Food has never been important to her. When she meets food writer and gourmand TREVOR, she falls hard for him.

On their first date she learns that he could never marry a woman who wasn't a gourmet chef. Realizing this could be deal-breaker, Grace reluctantly lies when he asks if she knows how to cook. She realizes that if she's going to have a future with Trevor, she must learn how to cook.

Act 2

Grace reads cookbooks, watches The Food Network and takes a cooking class. Because she has to learn fast, nothing's working. Meanwhile, Trevor's pressuring her to cook for him, which she keeps avoiding. He's also asking her esoteric questions about cooking that she either dodges or manages to answer because of the little bit of research she's done.

She's becoming a wreck in her attempt to avoid cooking for him and talking with him about food, which is his favorite subject. Trevor's getting suspicious. Then Grace gets a break. She finds out about a retired chef who specializes in quickly teaching people how to cook.

Grace also has a nemesis: DENISE, another food writer who has a thing for Trevor. After meeting Grace she's suspicious about her culinary talents.

Her new teacher puts Grace with two other people who need to learn to cook fast: RANDY, a firefighter who has just been named firehouse cook, and ELLIOT, a fat guy who's been told to lose weight or die. Grace, Randy, and Elliot bond. With Randy and Elliot's help Grace cooks a fine meal for Trevor. She figures the heat is off, but then Trevor asks her to cook Thanksgiving dinner for his friends and his boss, who will be alone on Thanksgiving. There's no way she can avoid it.

ACT 3

With Randy and Elliot's help Grace does a trial run cooking a Thanksgiving dinner. Trevor emphasizes how important the meal will be because he wants to impress his boss and get a promotion. She learns that his boss is the one who implanted in his head the importance of having a wife who cooks. Trevor remarks that it doesn't matter to him because he prefers to eat out anyway.

This upsets Grace. She realizes all the stuff she's gone through learning to cook was for naught. She's angry. She goes to Randy for advice. (NOTE: We'll have learned that Randy's had a crush on her throughout.) They go for a drink to talk about the situation. They pass a fine dining restaurant and see Trevor kissing another woman.

Grace wants to confront Trevor. Randy has a better idea: sabotage Thanksgiving dinner so Trevor won't get the promotion. The story ends with Randy and Grace getting together and with Grace realizing she's a good cook.

writing exercise

Do an Outline of an idea you have for a feature-length comedy. Start by following the example of *Smothered With Onions.*

writing exercise

Using either the outline in the previous exercise or a new idea, expand it following the format of *Dashing Through the Snow.*

writing exercise

If you've been working on the same outline or if you want to use a new idea, now write a three-act breakdown following the format of *Grace Before Meals.*

Note: Writing outlines and breakdowns of ideas that are still in your head is difficult. I've found over the years that most people find doing these things helpful. Some are better at it than others, but even if you find it frustrating at times, please stick with it. The more of them you do, the less difficult they become. Notice, I didn't say it gets "easier." It doesn't ever get easier, but with practice and skill and experience you won't have as hard a time writing them.

10 Terms You Might Already Know but if You Don't, You Should
(And Even if You Do, It Never Hurts to Brush Up on Them)

(1). Rule of 3: Things that come in threes are inherently funnier, more satisfying, or more effective than other numbers of things.

(2) Running Gag: A joke, situation, or line that repeats. Running gags may also be connected to an event that occurred previously.

(3) Sight Gag: A joke whose laugh is visual rather than verbal.

(4) Callback: A joke that refers to one previously told in a comedian's set, TV show, or movie. The second, third, and even fourth reference to it is often presented in a different context than the one used in the initial joke.

(5) Blow or Button: A final joke at the end of a scene.

(6) Cold Open or Teaser: A short scene that precedes the first act of a sitcom script. It appears before the opening credits.

(7) Fourth Wall: A theater term referring to an imaginary wall through which the audience watches the performance.

(8) Breaking the Fourth Wall: In a live play, an actor speaks directly to the audience. In a sitcom or movie, it's when an actor looks directly into the camera and seems to talk to the viewers.

(9) Punch Up: To take a joke or line already written and make it better, i.e., funnier.

(10) Tag: A short scene before or during the end credits.

167

chapter 15

Always
Leave Them Laughing

Try again. Fail Again. Fail Better.

— Samuel Beckett

Even though this book is about being funny, I want to end it on a serious note, so I won't leave you laughing.

Instead, I will leave you with a challenge. While humor may come easily to you in your daily life, trying to use that ability to earn a living won't.

WARNING!!!

Another cooking analogy.

Take someone who's a great cook. Everybody loves her food. Everybody encourages her to open a restaurant. So she figures, why not? She will quickly learn that being a great home cook does not guarantee success as a restaurateur. This is because being a great cook and running a successful restaurant are two different things.

The home cook only *cooks* at home. She's in her kitchen and only has to worry about the act of cooking.

The cook/chef/owner of a restaurant has to deal with many other problems like rent, salaries, equipment, staff, advertising, suppliers, equipment that breaks, alcoholic cooks, incompetent waiters, a bartender who steals, vermin, a broken freezer, lack of business, et al.

Trying to break into the world of comedy, no matter which venue you pursue, makes you like that home cook. Everybody laughs at your jokes now and tells you how funny you are and you *know* that you're funny and you can't stand your job and you feel confident that you have what it takes, so you take a deep breath and go for it.

But just like that home cook opening her new restaurant, there will be hurdles, setbacks, and disappointments for you along the way.

If you have thick skin, you have an advantage. If not, it's going to be tougher, so I urge you to learn how to be resilient.

Don't reject criticism. Welcome it. If someone offers you feedback, negative or positive, listen, *especially* if it's negative. Process it. If you're really lucky you'll have (or find) one person who won't bullshit you, who'll be brutally honest when you've written something bad or good.

Lastly, put the word "try" at the top of your vocabulary. And look at the Samuel Beckett quote above. Keep trying. If one thing doesn't work, try another. If that doesn't play, try something else. Keep trying until one day something feels right. It works. It's good. You know it's good and the person who's brutally honest with you says it's good.

That's a small victory.

And a good way to start the battle!

Laughter and tears are both responses to
frustration and exhaustion. I myself prefer to laugh,
since there is less cleaning up to do afterward.

— Kurt Vonnegut

About the Author

photo by Allison Maggy

D.B. GILLES has taught comedy writing in The Maurice Kanbar Institute of Film & Television at New York University's Tisch School of the Arts for nearly 20 years.

He also taught comedy in The Dramatic Writing Department at NYU, the Graduate Film Department at Columbia, The American Comedy Institute in New York City, and The Gallatin School of Individualized Study at NYU.

He is the author of *The Screenwriter Within* and *The Portable Film School.* He is co-author of the George Bush parody *W. The First Hundred Days. A White House Journal*.

D.B. is also a script consultant and writing coach. Many of his students have gotten deals, sold scripts, had their work published and their TV scripts, sketches, and screenplays produced.

He is the author of the popular blog *Screenwriters Rehab: For Screenwriters Who Can't Get Their Acts Together.*

You can reach D.B. Gilles for information about script consulting through his website:

screenwritingwithdbgilles.com

You can e-mail him directly at:

dbgillescript@gmail.com

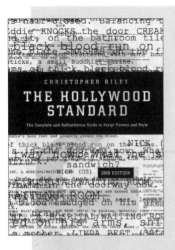

THE HOLLYWOOD STANDARD
2ND EDITION
THE COMPLETE AND AUTHORITATIVE GUIDE TO SCRIPT FORMAT AND STYLE

CHRISTOPHER RILEY

This is the book screenwriter Antwone Fisher (*Antwone Fisher*, *Tales from the Script*) insists his writing students at UCLA read. This book convinced John August (*Big Fish*, *Charlie and the Chocolate Factory*) to stop dispensing formatting advice on his popular writing website. His new advice: Consult *The Hollywood Standard*. The book working and aspiring writers keep beside their keyboards and rely on every day. Written by a professional screenwriter whose day job was running the vaunted script shop at Warner Bros., this book is used at USC's School of Cinema, UCLA, and the acclaimed Act One Writing Program in Hollywood, and in screenwriting programs around the world. It is the definitive guide to script format.

The Hollywood Standard describes in clear, vivid prose and hundreds of examples how to format every element of a screenplay or television script. A reference for everyone who writes for the screen, from the novice to the veteran, this is the dictionary of script format, with instructions for formatting everything from the simplest master scene heading to the most complex and challenging musical underwater dream sequence. This new edition includes a quick start guide, plus new chapters on avoiding a dozen deadly formatting mistakes, clarifying the difference between a spec script and production script, and mastering the vital art of proofreading. For the first time, readers will find instructions for formatting instant messages, text messages, email exchanges and caller ID.

"Aspiring writers sometimes wonder why people don't want to read their scripts. Sometimes it's not their story. Sometimes the format distracts. To write a screenplay, you need to learn the science. And this is the best, simplest, easiest to read book to teach you that science. It's the one I recommend to my students at UCLA."

— Antwone Fisher, from the foreword

CHRISTOPHER RILEY is a professional screenwriter working in Hollywood with his wife and writing partner, Kathleen Riley. Together they wrote the 1999 theatrical feature *After the Truth*, a multiple-award-winning German language courtroom thriller. Since then, the husband-wife team has written scripts ranging from legal and political thrillers to action-romances for Touchstone Pictures, Paramount Pictures, Mandalay Television Pictures and Sean Connery's Fountainbridge Films.

In addition to writing, the Rileys train aspiring screenwriters for work in Hollywood and have taught in Los Angeles, Chicago, Washington D.C., New York, and Paris. From 2005 to 2008, the author directed the acclaimed Act One Writing Program in Hollywood.

$24.95 · 208 PAGES · ORDER NUMBER 130RLS · ISBN: 9781932907636

YOUR SCREENPLAY SUCKS!
100 WAYS TO MAKE IT GREAT

WILLIAM M. AKERS

All beginning writers make the same mistakes – and many "pros" do, too! Because nobody in Hollywood will give your script a second chance, it better be perfect the first time out. No longer will you worry that a producer or story executive will toss your script in the garbage at page fifteen because *Your Screenplay Sucks!* Akers' checklist will eliminate all the flaws in your screenplay, guaranteeing a cover-to-cover read.

This book includes the most comprehensive checklist of fatal errors all writers make – and then provides the tools to fix them.

In today's highly competitive story market, this is the only book that finds the flaws in your script – like a heat-seeking missile – and shows you how to eliminate them.

"William M. Akers is a renaissance man of film who is at once a big studio writer, independent writer/director, and caring, insightful teacher. He also knows every trick in the book when it comes to fixing a script. And this is that book! A must for any writer facing 'the dark night of the script.'"
    – Blake Snyder, author, *Save the Cat!*®, *Save the Cat!*® *Goes to the Movies*

"Don't even think about writing a screenplay without reading Your Screenplay Sucks!!*"*
    – Linda McCullough, Columbia College Chicago

"A book about screenwriting that reads like a good screenplay. It is so full of great stories, examples and advice that I couldn't put it down."
    – Tom Schulman, Academy® Award-Winning screenwriter, *Dead Poets Society;* screenwriter, *Honey I Shrunk The Kids, What About Bob?*

A Lifetime Member of the Writer's Guild of America, WILLIAM AKERS has had three feature films produced from his screenplays. A writer/producer with 15 years experience, he has written feature scripts, series television, and documentaries for MGM, Disney, and Universal, as well as the Fox, NBC, ABC, TNN television networks. He received a Telly Award for directing and producing non-broadcast documentaries. He teaches screenwriting and filmmaking at Vanderbilt. His feature film, *105 Degrees and Rising*, about the fall of Saigon, is in pre-production.

$19.95 · 220 PAGES · ORDER NUMBER 85RLS · ISBN 13: 9781932907452

THE WRITER'S JOURNEY – 3RD EDITION
MYTHIC STRUCTURE FOR WRITERS

CHRISTOPHER VOGLER

BEST SELLER

See why this book has become an international best seller and a true classic. *The Writer's Journey* explores the powerful relationship between mythology and storytelling in a clear, concise style that's made it required reading for movie executives, screenwriters, playwrights, scholars, and fans of pop culture all over the world.

Both fiction and nonfiction writers will discover a set of useful myth-inspired storytelling paradigms (i.e., "The Hero's Journey") and step-by-step guidelines to plot and character development. Based on the work of Joseph Campbell, *The Writer's Journey* is a must for all writers interested in further developing their craft.

The updated and revised third edition provides new insights and observations from Vogler's ongoing work on mythology's influence on stories, movies, and man himself.

"This book is like having the smartest person in the story meeting come home with you and whisper what to do in your ear as you write a screenplay. Insight for insight, step for step, Chris Vogler takes us through the process of connecting theme to story and making a script come alive."
> – Lynda Obst, Producer, *Sleepless in Seattle, How to Lose a Guy in 10 Days*;
>   Author, *Hello, He Lied*

"This is a book about the stories we write, and perhaps more importantly, the stories we live. It is the most influential work I have yet encountered on the art, nature, and the very purpose of storytelling."
> – Bruce Joel Rubin, Screenwriter, *Stuart Little 2, Deep Impact,*
>   *Ghost, Jacob's Ladder*

CHRISTOPHER VOGLER is a veteran story consultant for major Hollywood film companies and a respected teacher of filmmakers and writers around the globe. He has influenced the stories of movies from *The Lion King* to *Fight Club* to *The Thin Red Line* and most recently wrote the first installment of *Ravenskull*, a Japanese-style manga or graphic novel. He is the executive producer of the feature film *P.S. Your Cat is Dead* and writer of the animated feature *Jester Till*.

$26.95 · 448 PAGES · ORDER NUMBER 76RLS · ISBN: 9781932907360

24 HOURS | 1.800.833.5738 | WWW.MWP.COM

THE MYTH OF MWP

In a dark time, a light bringer came along, leading the curious and the frustrated to clarity and empowerment. It took the well-guarded secrets out of the hands of the few and made them available to all. It spread a spirit of openness and creative freedom, and built a storehouse of knowledge dedicated to the betterment of the arts.

The essence of the Michael Wiese Productions (MWP) is empowering people who have the burning desire to express themselves creatively. We help them realize their dreams by putting the tools in their hands. We demystify the sometimes secretive worlds of screenwriting, directing, acting, producing, film financing, and other media crafts.

By doing so, we hope to bring forth a realization of 'conscious media' which we define as being positively charged, emphasizing hope and affirming positive values like trust, cooperation, self-empowerment, freedom, and love. Grounded in the deep roots of myth, it aims to be healing both for those who make the art and those who encounter it. It hopes to be transformative for people, opening doors to new possibilities and pulling back veils to reveal hidden worlds.

MWP has built a storehouse of knowledge unequaled in the world, for no other publisher has so many titles on the media arts. Please visit www.mwp.com where you will find many free resources and a 25% discount on our books. Sign up and become part of the wider creative community!

Onward and upward,

Michael Wiese
Publisher/Filmmaker